The Nigerian Capital Market: Developments, Issues and Policies

The Nigerian Capital Market:
Developments, Issues and Policies

Isaac Olusola Dada

Spectrum Books Limited
Ibadan
•Abuja • Benin City • Lagos • Owerri

Spectrum titles can be purchased on line at
www.spectrumbooksonline.com

Published by
Spectrum Books Limited
Spectrum House
Ring Road
PMB 5612
Ibadan, Nigeria
e-mail: admin1@spectrumbooksonline.com

in association with
Safari Books (Export) Limited
1st Floor
17 Bond Street
St Helier
Jersey JE2 3NP
Channel Islands
United Kingdom

Europe and USA Distributor
African Books Collective Ltd
The Jam Factory
27 Park End Street
Oxford OX1, 1HU, UK

First published 2003

ISBN: 978-029-344-2

Printed by Sam-Adex Printers, Felele Rab, Ibadan

Contents

Foreword

I am honoured that the author suggested that I write the foreword to this book – *The Nigerian Capital Market: Developments, Issues and Policies*. My reason for agreeing to do so is because the author has devoted an extraordinary amount of his time to researching, discussing, writing, rewriting and continuously polishing what you have in your hands, being the final product. Moreover, I have personally been involved, through research, education and training with the dissemination of knowledge about the capital market. The capital market is an area in which there appears to be an unquestionable thirst for knowledge and information from practitioners, investors and the general public. There has been a paucity of published material on the capital market in Nigeria. The book is written from a practitioner's perspective.

The primary focus of the book is on capital market development and it has been prepared from this standpoint. It chronicles the impact of regulation on the development of the Nigerian Capital Market. To that extent, many of the chapters were devoted to the analysis of the regulatory and operational guidelines in the Nigerian Capital Market. Students and practitioners will find the book of considerable benefit in understanding the evolution of the capital market and the role which regulation played in the orderly development of the market.

The book has drawn attention to the content of policies as they evolve in parallel line with market conditions. The book lays bare the development of policies with some degree of factual detail. The reader is invited to learn the nuts and bolts of some operational aspects of the Nigerian Capital Market particularly with respect to security trading and settlement, as a result of the introduction of the computerised trading and settlement system, otherwise known as the Central Securities Clearing System (CSCS). The CSCS is exhaustively discussed for the benefit of those interested in the operations and transactions system in the Nigerian Stock Exchange. The author shows how the introduction of the CSCS changed the transaction cycle from 6 months to 4 days and the inter-broker settlement from 14 days to 4 days (T+3), with significant impact on the volume and value of shares traded.

Similarly, another important development has been the automation of the stock market-process, effected through the replacement of the manual trading system – the call-over system - by an Automated Trading System (ATS).

Great progress has also been made toward understanding how the capital market functions, how securities are traded and how prices of financial instruments are determined. This book has taken advantage of the progress made in finance over the last three decades, by discussing at a fairly introductory level the conceptual issues in valuation of securities and the concepts of the cost of capital (chapters 8 and 9). These two chapters will be of benefit to undergraduate students and new recruits into the stockbroking business. The author examined the different types of bonds for financing government borrowing requirements (chapter 7). This chapter provides a breath of fresh air when compared to the "all-purpose or hybrid revenue bonds" being unleashed on the undiscerning investors by most Issuing Houses. In most cases, it is difficult, even for the most discerning investors, to determine whether a particular issue is really a revenue or a general obligation bond. The chapter casts an illumination which separates the "wheat from the tares" and thereby assisting market operators from further taking a walk in the woods.

Generally, the book is a collection of essays. The analysis presented is an outgrowth of many papers of different themes presented over the years at various conferences and seminars by the author, but many of which have undergone substantial modifications and improvement. The book also reflects the author's experience as an operator in the Nigerian Stock Market. While the primary focus is on issues relating to the development of the capital market, some of the essays (chapters 10 to 13) are only tangentially related to the principal theme though of no less value. Indeed, each of the topics examined deserves an in-depth treatment of its own. The author has only tried to outline the broad themes, but much more could be written on all these topics.

Prof. O. Akintola-Bello
Dean, Faculty of Management Sciences
Olabisi Onabanjo University
Ago – Iwoye, Ogun State, Nigeria.

and

Chairman, Arbitrage Consulting Group
Lagos, Nigeria.
March 14, 2003

Preface

The Nigerian Capital Market: Developments, Issues and Policies, is written to commemorate my sixtieth birthday anniversary which came up on 6th June, 2001. It is my contribution to the development of the Capital Market in Nigeria which turns out to be my professional interest area, after a career in the public sector and later in the banking sector of the Nigerian Economy.

The thought of writing a book on the Nigerian Capital Market had been on my mind since 1980 when I was privileged to be sent by the Federal Government of Nigeria to the prestigious IMF Institute in Washington D.C., USA, on a six month course on Financial Analysis and Policy. It is on record that officers around the world that are privileged to attend this specialised course usually end up either as Ministers of Finance or Governors of Central Banks of their various countries. Each participant in the programme is usually requested to write a dissertation on any issue of economic interest to his country. During my time at the IMF Institute, I was deeply touched by the need to develop the Capital Market in Nigeria so as to enhance economic development and promote private sector involvement as an engine of growth.

Providence, however, moved me from the public sector to the private sector in early 1993 when I started my banking career in NAL Merchant Bank Plc, as Executive Director, Corporate and Investment Banking Services. The movement further engendered my interest in the capital market. Early in my investment banking career, I had a bit of intensive training in Securities Market Management in Washington D.C., USA with the Intrados Management Group and the Faculty of Finance, George town University, in May 1993. My country paper presentation at the seminar is the first chapter of this book.

This book is thus a collection of papers, presented by me at different fora since 1993, arranged chronologically as they were delivered over time. Some issues raised in the earlier chapters of the book may have been overtaken by events, but I have decided not to edit such chapters in order to keep the authenticity of the papers as they were presented. However, the effects of later developments in the Nigerian Capital Market are also highlighted in the subsequent chapters, giving the book a developmental character.

The book is strictly not an academic text book. However, it is strongly hoped that issues dealt with in the book will be of immense benefit to various interest groups, such as students preparing for the examinations of the Chartered Institute of Stockbrokers, graduate and undergraduate students of Economics, Banking and Finance, Capital Market analysts and discerning investors.

It is with a deep sense of professional satisfaction that I present this book to the public.

Lagos.
January 2003

Chief I. Olusola Dada,
Executive Vice-Chairman,
Anchoria Investment & Securities Ltd.

Acknowledgements

I wish to express my sincere gratitude to all those colleagues of mine in the Nigerian Capital Market whose works I have benefited from in the course of writing the original papers which make up this book. My appreciation also goes to the two capital market regulatory bodies in Nigeria, namely, the Securities and Exchange Commission and the Nigerian Stock Exchange which are the institutional repositories of the various capital market regulations contained in this book.

Finally, I wish to express my deep appreciation to Mr. Gamaliel Onosode, the doyen of the Nigerian Capital Market and the immediate past President of the Chartered Institute of Stockbrokers of Nigeria, whose earlier advice after reading the draft of the book has made very significant contribution to producing a better book. I also say a big thank you to Prof. Olaseni Akintola-Bello, Dean, Faculty of Management Sciences, Olabisi Onabanjo University, Ago-Iwoye, Ogun State, Nigeria, who spent his valuable time in providing a foreword to the book after a critical appraisal of the manuscript. The same goes for Mr. Omotayo Adeyemo, Senior Research Manager at Anchoria Investment & Securities Limited, who proofread the manuscripts and Mrs. Dupe Akeredolu, my Personal Secretary, who typed the manuscripts. Also, my special love goes to my wife, 'Lola, and our children for giving me the required support. I take full responsibility for any error of omission or commission in this book.

Chapter One

Securities Market Management in an Emerging Market*

Introduction

This topic is of particular importance and relevance to Nigeria's economy, where changes in economic policies, such as deregulation, debt conversion, privatisation and commercialisation of government-owned enterprises, as well as interest rate deregulation, dominate the economic scene.

It will be necessary to trace the background of the Nigerian Securities Market and supportive government policies – regulatory environment, listing requirements, rules and regulations for operating firms, trading system as well as delivery and settlement procedures, in chronological order. Also, major securities as well as the problems and prospects of the market will be discussed. The term "Securities Market" is synonymous with Stock Market in Nigeria, and for this paper we shall be limited to the latter.

The Background of the Nigerian Stock Market

The idea to have a stock market in Nigeria dates back to the late fifties when the Federal Ministry of Industries set up a committee to advise it on ways and means of setting up a Stock Market.

Following the enthusiasm of local industries to raise fund from the public, it was thought that without a secondary market, this hope could not be realistically achieved. The desire for a Stock Exchange where trading in secondary securities could take place, therefore gained the attention of the industrial sector.

Paper presented in Washington DC., USA, at a Capital Market seminar organised by Intrados Management Group and Georgetown University, May, 1993.

1

Establishment of the Stock Exchange in Nigeria

The Nigerian Stock Exchange, formerly known as The Lagos Stock Exchange was incorporated in September 15, 1960. On 5th June, 1961, the Exchange commenced operations with three industrial securities, two federal government bonds and seven other securities which were subject to UK stamps duty.

The three important objectives for the incorporation of the exchange are:

(a) "To provide facilities to the public in Nigeria for the purchase and sale of funds, stocks and shares of any kind and the investment of money".

(b) "To control the granting of a quotation on the Lagos Stock Exchange in respect of funds, shares, or stock of any Company, Government, Municipalities, Local Authority or any other Corporation".

(c) "To correlate the Stockbroking activities of members, facilitate the exchange of information for their mutual advantage for the benefit of their clients, and to offer facilities whereby the public can be informed of the prices of shares dealt in by members".

These objectives still remained relevant in the operations of the capital market

Chronological Development of the Nigerian Capital Market

The Lagos Stock Exchange Act 1961

This Act gave legal backing to The Lagos Stock Exchange. In particular, it restricted the business of dealing in stocks and shares to members of the Stock Exchange. Other relevant enactments that support and regulate the operations of the market are discussed below.

Nigerian Enterprises Promotion Decree 1972

Government efforts at increasing the low level of activities in the market and promoting local capital formation, savings and investment in the industrial and commercial activities of the country, led to the promulgation of the Nigeria Enterprises Promotion Decree 1972. Following the promulgation of the Decree, twenty-three enterprises were listed on the Nigerian Stock Exchange.

Nigerian Enterprises Promotion Decree 1977

As a result of the effectiveness of the Nigeria Enterprises Promotions Decree of 1972, in promoting local capital formation and participation of Nigeria's industrial and commercial activities, and in particular, the impact on the capital market, government promulgated another decree in 1977. Under the new decree, enterprises were classified into three categories instead of the former two categories.

Under the 1977 Decree, all enterprises in Schedule One were exclusively reserved for Nigerians. Schedule Two specified enterprises in which Nigerians have 60% share participation, while Schedule Three indicated enterprises in which 40% share participation was reserved for Nigerians.

The Securities and Exchange Commission Decree 1979

This decree established the Nigerian Securities and Exchange Commission as the apex institution for the capital market. Under this decree, the Securities and Exchange Commission is empowered to register the Stock Exchange, or its branches, registrars, investment advisers, securities dealers and their agencies, as well as control and supervise their activities with a view to maintaining proper standard of conduct and professionalism in the securities business.

Nigerian Enterprises Promotion Decree 1989

In 1989, government promulgated another decree, the Nigerian Enterprises Promotion Decree 1989 through which government took a bold step to encourage foreign investors to have meaningful investment in the country. The 1989 Decree re-classified all enterprises in Nigeria into one Schedule and exclusively reserved for Nigerians, but also allowed alien participation in enterprises in cases where the capitalisation is not less than N20 million.

Privatisation and Commercialisation

Furthermore, in a bid to encourage foreign investors to participate in the economy, the federal government initiated a policy to shift the focus of the economy from government-dominated economy to private-sector led economy. The main objectives of this policy shift were to:

(i)   Develop the Nigerian Capital Market (The Capital Market).

(ii)   Re -structure the capital of relevant enterprises in order to facilitate good management and independent access to the capital market.

(iii)   Check the present absolute dependence on the treasury for funding by otherwise commercially oriented parastatals and to encourage their approach to the Capital Market

Management of the Stock Market in Nigeria

The supervision and management of the Stock Market are under the Securities and Exchange Commission, (SEC) and The Nigerian Stock Exchange (NSE) respectively. Two other government bodies, namely, the Federal Ministry of Finance and the Central Bank of Nigeria provide additional regulations in terms of official guidelines, monetary policies and special directives. The discussions in this paper will be limited to the SEC and the NSE because of their direct responsibilities for supervising and managing the Stock Market in Nigeria.

The Roles of the Securities and Exchange Commission

The SEC is the regulatory authority for the Nigerian Capital Market. It derives all its powers from the SEC Decree of 1979 and the revised Decree No. 29 of 1988. Like any other Securities and Exchange Commission in the world, it has the dual role of regulating as well as developing the capital market. The principal objectives of SEC Decree include:

1.   To promote the growth and development of the Nigerian Capital Market.

2.   To protect the interest of investors by preventing abuses in the market place and enhance confidence in the capital markets.

   To effectively carry out the above objectives, the commission is vested with the following roles under Section 6 of the SEC Decree.

(a)   Determining the amount of the price and time at which securities of a company are sold to the public either through offer for sale or subscription. (The powers of the SEC with regards to pricing under this section has been transferred to the Issuing Houses in the recent SEC guidelines on the deregulation of the capital market).

(b)   Registering all securities proposed to be offered for sale to or for subscription by the public, or to offer privately with the intention that securities shall be held ultimately other than by those whom the offers were made.

(c)   Maintaining surveillance over the dealing in the securities.

(d)   Registering Stock Exchanges or other branches, registrars, investment advisers, securities dealers and their agents, and controlling and supervising their activities with a view to maintaining proper standards of conduct and professionalism in the securities business.

(e)   Protecting the integrity of the securities market against any abuse arising from the practice of insider trading.

(f)   Acting as regulatory apex organisation for the Nigerian Capital Market including the Nigerian Stock Exchange and its branches to which it would be at liberty to delegate powers.

(g)   Reviewing, approving and regulating mergers, acquisitions and all forms of business combinations.

(h)   Creating the necessary atmosphere for the orderly growth and development of the capital market.

(i)   Undertaking such other activities as are necessary or expedient for giving full effects to the provisions of this decree.

The Nigerian Stock Exchange

The Nigerian Stock Exchange (NSE) is another important regulatory body in the Nigerian Capital Market. It is the pivot of the development in the Nigerian Capital Market in terms of providing avenues for investments and divestment in diverse stocks and shares. Like any other Stock Exchange in the world, the NSE is an organised market.

Membership

As a control measure, the NSE registers all its members which are classified into Ordinary and Dealing members. The Ordinary members of The Exchange are mainly Merchant and Commercial Banks and/or individuals, while Dealing members are mainly Stockbroking firms and individuals who are authorised clerks.

Regulation of Securities Firms

Securities firms or stockbrokers, as they are commonly called in Nigeria, are under the supervision of the Securities and Exchange Commission and The Nigerian Stock Exchange. The capital market is the market for long-term debt and equity securities hence it is synonymous with the securities market.

We serialise below the mechanism employed by the Exchange to regulate the activities of the market operators. The operators, principally stockbrokers, are regulated by the rules and regulations of the Exchange. The NSE has a code of conduct as well as rules and regulations. It also regulates the fees and commission of the Dealing members.

Rules and Regulations of The Nigerian Stock Exchange

The following are extracts of the regulation:

1. These regulations shall be binding upon members in their relationship to the Exchange, as between themselves as Dealing members and regulating the business which they conduct as members of the Exchange with the general public.

2. It is the duty of every Dealing member of the Exchange to observe these regulations and to report forthwith any breach of the Articles or Regulations by any other member in writing to the branch councils of the Nigerian Stock Exchange Council, otherwise the member shall be guilty of these regulations.

3. The names of all partners or directors of any firm or company under which a member carried on stockbroking business or which is a member, shall be printed upon all letter-heads, contract notes, pamphlets or other documents used by the members in the transaction of such business.

4. No member of the Exchange (other than a member acting under the specific authority of either Council) shall hold himself out to any person as being the agent of or otherwise representing or having the power in any way to act for or bind the Exchange.

5. Members shall notify the Secretary, Nigerian Stock Exchange in writing the address of any office, or offices in Nigeria at which they intend to carry on stockbroking business before commencing such business.

6. Members of the Exchange shall not canvass for business and shall only be permitted to exhibit outside offices at which they carry on stockbroking business in plate bearing the name in which business is carried on, of a size not larger than 12 inches by 6 inches, or if a circular plate, with diameter not exceeding 9 inches.

7. No member shall institute legal proceedings to enforce a claim against another member arising out of stockbroking transactions without the consent of the council.

8. Every Dealing member shall keep all monies held on behalf of

clients in a bank account separate from that kept by the member for his or its own monies and such account shall be kept in the name in which the member carried on his or its stockbroking business followed by the words "Client's Account."

9. Every Dealing member shall keep proper records and books of account in respect of all stockbroking transactions. The council shall prescribe the forms in which such records and books are to be kept by Members and be entitled to appoint the Secretary or Committee to inspect the records of members from time to time and report thereon to the council.

10. When required by the council, a Dealing member shall supply to it a statutory declaration (in such form as the council may prescribe) of his private financial position.

11. Any member who shall have a transaction with another member in which each other member shall make default shall forthwith notify the secretary in writing of such default.

12. No member shall compromise with or accept any payment on account from any member in connection with any transaction.

    Any member so compromising with or accepting payment on account from any other member shall, in the event of such other member being declared a defaulter within six months from the dáte of such compromise or payment be liable at the discretion of the council to pay or make over to the Exchange any monies or securities received from the defaulters at the time of and subsequent to such compromise or payment on account.

13. In all cases of default, the Council shall meet and appoint a committee which shall have the following powers:

    (a) To engage technical and professional assistance.

    (b) To require from the defaulter his original books of account relating to, and a statement of sums owing to and by him in connection with stockbroking transactions.

    (c) To call meetings of members who are creditors of the defaulters.

(d)   To summon the defaulter to appear before such meetings and meetings of the committee.

(e)   To make detailed examinations of all relative accounts.

(f)   To report to the council any transaction or matter which may appear to be or have been irregular.

(g)   To apply monies paid to securities made over to the Exchange under Regulation 12 thereof.

(h)   Otherwise to manage and deal with the stockbroking business of the defaulter and the assets thereof in conformity with the Articles and any Regulations which may be made hereunder and with the customs and usages of the stockbroking profession.

14.   A defaulter shall, when called upon to do so in terms of paragraph 13 of these regulations, hand over to the committee all books, accounts and documents connected with his stockbroking business, a statement of all sums owing to and by him in connection with such business at the time of the default and any other relevant documents and information which the committee may require.

15.   Any Member who shall be declared a defaulter or be adjudicated bankrupt shall forthwith cease to be a member.

16.   Any application by any company for a quotation of its shares on the Exchange must be sponsored by a member and made in such form as may be prescribed by the council from time to time.

17.   The Council shall not grant a quotation for the shares of any company unless it has conformed with the requirements as laid down from time to time by the council.

18.   The fee for a quotation of a company's share in the Official List (as hereinafter defined) conformed with the requirements as laid down by the council from time to time.

19.   The quotation of any share may be cancelled or suspended without giving any reason for such decision.

20.   No dealing, except as provided by the Regulation 21, will be allowed in any issue of stocks or shares other than securities

for which permission to deal has been granted by The Nigerian Stock Exchange or as may currently appear in the Official List.

21. In the case of the securities not falling within that described in Regulation 20, specific bargains may be made with the permission of the council. Application for such permission must be made in the form prescribed by the council.

22. The branch Exchanges shall open for dealing at such days except Saturdays, Sundays and public holidays, and during such hours as the branch council shall decide.

23. Any offer to buy or sell stock or at a price named when no quantity is named is binding to the amount of 100 shares or units, except when the offer is to deal in a parcel, which shall be deemed to consist of not less than 200 or more than 500 shares or in odd quantities, the number of shares or units must be named.

24. When shares or stocks have been duly tendered and are not paid for in conformity with the terms of the sale, the seller shall have the right to cause the shares or stocks to be sold out and any loss occasioned thereby shall be paid by the buyer.

25. The seller of stock or shares for cash shall make or tender delivery within a reasonable time but not later than 2 days after the day on which the transaction has been made. Delivery shall in all cases be made or tendered at the office of the broker effecting the purchase, on a business day or at least one hour before bank closing time on that day.

26. Unless otherwise prescribed by the council:

    (i) Any securities in the Official List with a Local Register shall be marked ex-dividend on the day nearest to that fourteen days prior to the date on which the register is closed for transfers.

    (ii) Any security, in the Official List, in respect of which the register is maintained outside Nigeria shall be marked ex-dividend on the day on which it is so marked by the recognised Stock Exchange on which the security is primarily quoted.

(iii)   Any fixed interest securities quoted in the Official List shall be marked ex-interest on the day nearest to that seven days prior to the date on which the Register is closed for transfers.

27. No Member shall submit for registration any transfer relating to the purchase of a security, dealt in ex-dividend, until the relative Register of Transfer Books have been closed for payment of such dividend.

28. Every year the council shall fix period of Settlement of Account amongst Dealing members which will be operative for that calendar year.

29. Penalty for default in meeting the conditions of the Settlement of Account Scheme shall be as prescribed from time to time.

Listing Requirements of The Exchange

The NSE maintains quotation for large, medium and small scale enterprises. The term quotation is synonymously used with the term listed, but this entitles the securities to be traded on The Exchange.

For the purpose of being listed on The Exchange, a company must belong to the First or the Second-Tier Securities Market. Large and medium size companies are listed on the First-Tier Market while small-scale industries are listed on the Second-Tier Securities Market.

Conditions for Quotation

(The First-Tier Securities Market)

The NSE prescribed different conditions for the market as follows:

(a) It must have been in existence for five years with audited accounts for each of the years.

(b) At the time of making application, the date of latest audited figures must not be more than nine months.

(c) Not less than 25% or ₦250,000 of the issued share capital must be made available to the public.

(d) The amount that can be raised is limitless depending on the borrowing powers of the company.

(e) Companies in this category are required to submit quarterly, half-yearly and annual statements of account.

(f) The number of shareholders must not be less than 100.

The Second-Tier Securities Market

To be listed in this segment of the Market:

(a) The company must have been in existence for three years with audited accounts for each of the years.

(b) At the time of making application, the latest audited accounts must not be less than nine months.

(c) At least 10% or ₦50,000 of the equity capital of the company must be made available to the public.

(d) The amount that can be raised may not exceed ₦10,000,000 (Ten Million Naira).

(e) Companies in this category are required to submit quarterly, half-yearly and annual statements of account.

(f) The number of shareholders must not be less than 100.

Review of Capital Market Operations

Over the years, there have been increasing calls on relevant authorities for modification of the nation's economic policies as they affect the entire capital market with a view to:

(i)   reducing excessive controls in order to allow market forces to create a more competitive and efficient economy;

(ii)   increasing the flow of information to reduce uncertainties, insider dealings and allow investors to take firm investment decisions and have greater confidence in the market;

(iii) increasing the number of operators in the market and create room for competition and efficiency in the provision of financial services; and

(iv) removing controls on the allocation of the nation's scarce resources to permit efficient utilisation by the productive sector and bring about the necessary linkages for the use of capital market funds.

Trading System of the Nigerian Stock Market

The stock market in Nigeria operates the Call-Over System. Transactions in the market are carried out by licensed stockbrokers. The market is provided and supervised by The Exchange at any of the six trading floors which are located in Lagos, Port Harcourt, Kano, Kaduna, Onitsha, and Ibadan.

Documents for Trading in the Stock Market

The following are the main documents for trading in the stock market:

The Daily Official List

This is a document which is published daily by the authority of the Council of The Exchange. This document contains information on all quoted companies with regards to price, quotation, maturity date, date of last dividend/interest and rate, earnings per share etc.

The Bargain Slip

This is the binding receipt issued by dealers and exchanged between themselves on the trading floor for consummated transactions.

The Jobbing Book

The Jobbing Book contains a record of the various quantities of shares and stocks to be sold and/or purchased on the floor by the Dealer. It is the book that guides the activities of the Dealer in the market.

Composition and Procedure for Trading in the Stock Market

The market comprises the following participants: officials of The Exchange, made up of the Chairman of Call-Over, and the Call-Over Clerks, accredited representatives of each of the stockbroking firms. Members of the public and the press as well as a representative of the Securities and Exchange Commission are usually in attendance, as observers.

Trading in the market is commenced with the Chairman calling the Call-Over to order, and immediately, the Call-Over Clerk calls each of the Securities on the Official List. As the business of the day progresses, prices are made, Dealers indicate Offer and Bid interests and deals are struck. A deal is struck when there is an offer and a bid and the Chairman of Call-Over distributes the shares on offer among the bidding stockbrokers.

Delivery and Settlement Procedure

Delivery

In order to ensure high degree of integrity and discipline among stockbroking firms, the Nigerian Stock Exchange makes it mandatory that:

> The seller of a stock or shares for cash shall make or tender delivery within a reasonable time, say not later than 21 days, after the day on which the transaction has been made. Delivery shall in all cases be made or tendered at the office of the broker effecting the purchase on a business day and at least one hour before bank closing time on that day.

All arrangements with regards to authentication of transfers by The

Exchange and Certification by the Registrars must therefore be completed within the prescribed 21-day period to facilitate compliance.

Authentication by The Exchange

Authentication or Noting as it is otherwise called, is obtained by a Stockbroker when the Stockbroker presents the sellers and brokers Share Transfer Forms, in connection with a previous day's transaction, to The Exchange for approval.

The Exchange gives approval or authenticates the transaction, when it applies the Official Stamp to the reverse side of the Share Transfer Form and the Signature of the Secretary to the Council of the Exchange or any other accredited representative of The Exchange is applied on the document.

There are two types of deliveries; the Direct Delivery and Delivery by Certification.

Delivery by Certification

Certification is the process of initiating instrument of delivery (Share Transfer Form) by the Selling Broker in favour of the Buying Broker so that the Selling Broker can deliver the shares sold to the Buying Broker. The Share Transfer Form, prepared in the name of the Buying Broker with the number of shares stated on it, becomes an instrument of delivery after the Registrar has certified (with the aid of stamp and signature) that it has in its custody Transfer Form. The Transfer Form is then delivered to the Buying Broker by the Selling Broker.

Direct Delivery

Direct delivery is made when all the shares covered by a Share Certificate are purchased by a single Broker. The Selling Broker will deliver the seller's (client's) Share Transfer Form and the Certificate to the Buying Broker so that the latter can transfer the shares to its client (buyer). It is noteworthy that brokers simply buy and sell shares on behalf of their clients in Nigeria.

Settlement

For the purpose of settlement, the council of The Exchange shall fix the period of Settlement of Account among Dealing members which will operate for a calendar year.

In this regard, the year is divided into fifty two (52) settlement periods and transactions for the past two weeks are settled in the next two weeks falling on a Friday.

The settlement is usually done by cheque or bank draft drawn by the Buying Broker to the Selling Broker. The Council of the Exchange also prescribes penalties for default which range from the payment of fine, suspension, to withdrawal of Dealing licence.

Major Securities Traded in the Market

Major securities traded in the stock market include: Equities, Preference Shares, Industrial Loan Stocks, State and Local Government Bonds and the Federal Republic of Nigeria Development Stock.

Equities

These are ordinary shares of a company listed on the First and Second-Tier Markets of the Exchange. The nominal value of the shares range between 20k and 100k. Trading in the securities is carried out on every working day.

As at May 1993, there were 140 equities of companies listed in the First-Tier Market, while 21 equities were quoted in the Second-Tier Market.

Preference Shares

Preference shares are also traded in the market, though they are very rare. They are usually issued by various companies and are similar to industrial loans stock in the sense that, they carry a fixed interest and are sometimes convertible into ordinary shares. Some preference shares do not carry maturity dates.

Industrial Loans

Industrial loans are issued by companies or industries and may carry a fixed or floating interest rate, with a maturity date. The issuer, a company, usually provides a Sinking Fund arrangement for the retirement of the loan stock. The stocks are usually issued at par and interests are paid bi-annually on the stock. They are usually project – tied. There were 58 of such stocks on the Exchange as at the end of May, 1993.

Local Government Bonds

These are usually issued at the instance of the Local Government authorities. In the case of Local Government Bond, it is usually guaranteed by the granted autonomy to raise funds from the Capital Market. They are usually project-tied (or mostly revenue bonds) and have all the features of an Industrial Loan Stock.

State Bonds

These are issued in the same manner as Local Government Bonds and are also project – tied (revenue bonds) and have all the features of Industrial Loan Stocks. There are five of such stocks listed on the Exchange today.

Federal Government Stock

These are issued for development purposes and are project-tied. They are issued and managed by the Central Bank of Nigeria on behalf of the Federal Government. They are Gilt-edge Stocks, which have remained the most attractive among the stocks listed on the Exchange because of the ease of convertibility to cash. They are fixed interest stocks with dates of maturity, while interests are paid bi-annually. They are usually issued in tranches. As at the time of writing this paper, there are thirty-six of such stocks listed on The Exchange.

Problems Facing the Stock Market Today

Some of the problems facing the Market today include:

(a)   Delay in the issuance of certificates.

(b)   Lack of adequate flow of information.

(c)   The buy and hold attitude of investors which create artificial scarcity in the Market.

(d)   Low level of awareness among the investing public.

Prospects

Over the years, The Exchange embarked on some measures aimed at improving the stock market. The measures include:

Internationalisation of the Stock Market

Information on every trading day with regard to the names, share prices, quantity of shares traded and others on all the quoted companies listed on The Exchange are beamed worldwide via the Communications Network. This measure is designed to disseminate information on quoted companies to foreign, private and portfolio investors regarding the Nigerian Stock Market. Therefore to fully internationalise the stock market, the foreign investors are needed to participate in the Secondary Market.

Improved Delivery System

An improved delivery system is required to reduce the long delays often associated with the issuance of Share Certificates. It is hoped that the establishment of a Central Security-Clearing System, being sponsored by The Exchange and the private sector, will bring about a fast and efficient service with regards to certification and issuance of certificates to investors.

Chapter Two

The Nigerian Capital Market: Opportunities and Challenges*

What is Capital Market

The capital market exists to provide long-term capital to both government and corporate bodies for industrial, socio-economic and infrastructural development purposes. The capital market deals with financing instruments of long-term nature. These instruments include equities (ordinary shares) and bonds. The capital market is different from the money market in terms of the maturity profile of the instruments issued and traded. The money market essentially consists of short-tenure instruments, often of less than one-year maturity such as bankers' acceptance, commercial papers and treasury bills.

The capital market operates at two levels – the primary market where new issues or securities are raised from the investing public, with proceeds going to the issuer, and the secondary market where old or outstanding securities are bought and sold. The secondary market provides liquidity and marketability and thus ensures the efficiency of the primary market.

In view of the flexibility of the capital market in terms of instruments, it ensures that the investment preferences of both lenders and borrowers are satisfied.

The participants in the capital market can be broadly classified into four:

    i.   Providers of funds (investor-individuals, unit trust, and other corporate bodies).

Paper Presented at the Management Training Seminar Organised by AIESEC, at the Nigerian Institute of Advanced Legal Studies, University of Lagos, Akoka, Lagos in June, 1998.

19

ii.   Users of funds (companies and governments).

iii.   Intermediaries (facilitator-stockbroking firms, issuing houses, Registrars).

iv.   Regulators (Securities and Exchange Commission, The Nigerian Stock Exchange).

As could be seen, while the providers of funds essentially comprise individuals and companies, the users of funds (issuer of securities) include companies and governments. In other words, individuals may not be able to raise money from the capital market as they do in money market.

In this network of relationships, the Stock Exchange plays a central and indispensable role for which it has been variously described as the "hallmark or "heart" of the capital market. This is so because, even though in its strict definition, the Stock Exchange is a market for trading on outstanding issues, the opportunity which it offers for subsequent trading in existing securities has made it a decisive factor in the success or otherwise of many corporate issues and, by extension, the efficiency of capital formation in the economy. Thus, the availability of a secondary market engenders capital formation and socio-economic development.

Opportunities in the Nigerian Stock Market

The development of the capital market has entailed a number of benefits for the Nigerian economy. These benefits are in line with the general role of Stock Markets in the development process.

One, the stock market is a ready source of capital for the corporate sector. With current market capitalisation of about US$4 billion, the market stands out as a viable mechanism for resource mobilisation. For ten years up to the end of 1996, a cumulative total of ₦32 billion was raised by companies from the stock market. In 1996, the value of new issues amounted to ₦5.8 billion, a significant part of which was foreign portfolio investment.

The mere presence of a stock market in the country is a boost to the international investment climate of the country, as it raises the chances of additional local financing for both foreign and local direct investment. In an economy like Nigeria, where the banking sector is battling with credibility problem following the systemic distress of the financial sector, the stock market plays a morale boosting role to investors. It can only be imagined what the investment in the real sector would have been if the stock market had not been in place.

Two, the stock market provides opportunity for investment diversification. In the absence of the stock market, a large part of the wealth currently invested in the Nigerian Stock Market (about US$ 4 billion) would have been diverted to foreign countries. The market further remains a viable institution for holding back capital flight which has been identified as one of the causes of the country's economic underdevelopment.

Three, a major role for the stock market relates to the privatisation exercise. Privatisation of public enterprises, a cardinal plank of the Structural Adjustment Programme in many developing countries, aims at reducing the size of the public sector and correspondingly increasing private sector activities in the economies.

The successful implementation of the divestiture programmes offers a unique opportunity to underscore the importance of the stock market. The market played an unrivalled role in the implementation of the privatisation exercise as it did during the implementation of the indigenisation programme. Between 1988 and 1992, 35 enterprises were privatised through public offer of shares. The offers totalled 1.2 billion shares valued at ₦1.5 billion. This represented 5% of the market capitalisation in 1992.

To the general public, the exercise created awareness of the investment opportunity in the capital market, attracting 0.8 million new shareholders, amounting to a 200% increase in the number of new shareholders. The gains to the economy in terms of efficient operation of the privatised enterprises and relief to Government of the burden of subvention of the firms are some of the contributions of the exchange to the economy.

The stock market also enabled mass participation in the privatisation exercise and thus ensured that larger number of Nigerians benefited from ownership of the divested assets than would have ever been achieved in the absence of a stock market. It should be noted that even without economic growth, a more equitable distribution of wealth which the exercise facilitated is a desirable end in the quest for economic development. In other words, in the absence of a Stock Market, the sale of public wealth through privatisation would have benefited only a few rich persons, thereby worsening income inequality.

Challenges Now and in the Next Millennium

Nigeria has become an important market in the emerging economies chart of the world. However, her performance still falls below that of countries like Taiwan, South Africa, Malaysia, Korea, Brazil and India in terms of market capitalisation and turnover. Despite the fact that Nigeria has recorded over three decades of trading in securities, and having achieved an overwhelming growth in the market in the last decades, the system and procedures in the stock market are archaic and out of tune with international standards.

Therefore, to develop a proper perspective for appreciating the developments in the Nigerian Capital Market, it may be appropriate to briefly identify the shortcomings and deficiencies in the system before discussing the landmark changes witnessed in recent times.

Shortcoming/Deficiencies in the System

Physical Transfer of Scripts

The major shortcoming was the hitherto settlement system, necessitating physical transfer of stocks. This resulted in enormous paper work, bad and improper delivery of stocks and delays in registration and transfer of scripts. Objections raised during registration of transfer resulted in further delay in settlements.

Lack of depth and breadth

The growth of the Nigerian Capital Market over the last two decades has largely been confined to very few cities, notably Lagos, Kaduna, Kano and Port-Harcourt. In most of these cities, there has been relative lack of liquidity. Due to lack of information, investors in rural areas have not been able to exploit the full potentials in the capital market.

Lack of Market-Making

Only rudimentary kind of market- making is performed by illegal jobbers in the Nigerian Stock Market whereas, market makers with defined market-making responsibilities have traditionally been an integral part of the trading mechanism, an arrangement practised at the New York and London Stock Exchanges.

Lack of Infrastructure

The Nigerian Capital Market is faced with the problem of inadequate infrastructural facilities, such as effective computerization, telecommunication system, etc., resulting in lower operational efficiency.

Landmark Changes Witnessed in Recent Times

One of the economic policies of the 1998 budget was the repeal of all laws inhibiting competition. This had led to the establishment of a legal committee with the task of identifying such laws. Twelve of such laws were identified for amendment or abrogation in 1998, including laws governing capital market operations. It is in this spirit that government has decided to reform and modernize the Nigerian Capital Market, making it more responsive to the demand and challenges of the new millennium . Arising from these measures, government announced in its 1998 budget that the Abuja Stock Exchange would commence or be established in 1998. Government further directed that the Central Bank of Nigeria (CBN), National Insurance Corporation of Nigeria (NICON) and other interested private sector organizations should take steps to implement the decision.

In 1996, the Honourable Minister of Finance, had set up a panel under the Chairmanship of Chief Dennis Odife, to review the Nigerian Capital Market. Although neither the report of the panel nor the government white paper to that effect has been released, some aspects of the report that have become public knowledge are set below:

(i)   Proposal to set up a new Stock Exchange and rename the current Stock Exchange;

(ii)   Issues of Administration and Governance of the Stock Exchange in particular and the capital market in general and;

(iii) Urgent need to achieve rapid growth in virtually every dimension of the capital market (number of securities, volumes and values issued and traded, etc.).

The Federal Government had taken bold steps to introduce fundamental changes in the capital market. The changes, some of which were stated earlier, were essentially aimed at promoting the operational efficiency of the market, enhancing its competitiveness and responsiveness, fostering its internationalisation, improving the regulatory environment, and in general, deepening and broadening the market. Certainly, the proposed reforms would place the market on a better footing to cope with the socio-economic developmental needs and aspirations of the nation in the 21st century.

With the expected or planned high economic growth rate and the development of a strong entrepreneurial spirit in the new millennium, one expects to see considerable fund raising activities by corporations and governments. This would put pressure on the capital market to meet the long-term capital requirements of these entities. Such fund requirements are not likely to be restricted to the domestic market but access to the international capital markets are also anticipated. Similarly, the internationalisation of the market could bring about listings and capital sourcing by foreign issuers in Nigeria. In other words, the millennium is expected to usher-in cross-border issuance and listing activities. While many Nigerian companies may not currently qualify for listing on major stock markets partly because of financial disclosure requirements, the expected changes in the local environment should strengthen them in the early years of the 21st century to enter the international capital market for listings and funds.

A market which lacks liquidity would equally lack appeal. There is no gainsaying the fact that a major challenge which would face the market in the 21st century is the creation of a highly liquid market in which investors can buy and sell with relative ease, and large transactions absorbed without significant change in prices. A liquid market promotes professionalism and institutionalisations, as well as the deepening of a stock market.

Although with new listings and increased awareness, liquidity has over the decade improved, a lot more is still required to achieve the desirable level of liquidity. The present clearing and settlement of trades at T + 5 is commendable, but a shortened (T +3 or better) trade clearing and settlement period should be aimed at. This, coupled with investors' confidence in, and acceptance of an immobilised and dematerialised system as provided by the Central Securities Clearing System (CSCS), would, without doubt, bolster liquidity. In addition, the expected new listings by both local and foreign entities would broaden investment choices and stimulate activities in the Stock Market. New listings must thus be vigorously encouraged through incentives, reduced cost of accessing the market, the proposed Capital Trade Points, increased public awareness and the further strengthening of confidence in the market. It should be reiterated that the Lagos Stock Exchange Act 1960, should be repealed to bring all transactions in gilt-edged securities to the floor of the Stock Exchange.

One measure which needs to be taken to help deepen the capital market is the introduction of derivatives. Although some steps have been taken in this regard, one expects that traditional derivatives such as futures and options would be an integral part of the market in the 21st century. Derivatives such as index futures and options on individual stock, in particular, are expected to be widely and actively traded in the country thereby providing hedging and speculative opportunities to players.

By the year 2010, a well developed over-the-counter (OTC) market should be operational, to enable public unquoted companies to raise capital for expansion and facilitate secondary trading in the securities of such companies.

Conclusion

The report of the Vision 2010 Committee on the Nigerian Capital Market succinctly summarises the problem of the Nigerian Capital Market as follows:

> "the Nigerian Capital Market is small relative to the economy it is supposed to serve. It is shallow, unsophisticated and uncompetitive as a primary source of long-term business finance".

In order to enhance its role in the national economy and transform it into the engine of growth and a leading capital market in Africa, the following market related problems/issues need to be addressed:

(i)   Expansion of the market size relative to the economy;

(ii)   Transparency in the determination of price and other terms;

iii)   Efficiency of trading, settlement and delivery system;

(iv)   Liquidity;

(v)   Cost of doing business in both primary and secondary markets;

(vi)   Automation of operations;

(vii)   Widening the participation of Nigerians in the market;

(viii) Internationalisation, and the

(ix)   Dynamism of the regulatory framework.

References

1. Alile, H.L.

"The Stock Exchange and Capital Formation in Nigeria". Paper presented at the Senior Executive Course No. 19 of The Nigerian Institute for Policy and Strategic Studies, Kuru. March 1997.

2. Dada, I.O.

"Role of Domestic and International Capital Market in the Recapitalisaton of Banks in Nigeria". Paper presented at The Workshop organised by the Chartered Institute of Bankers of Nigeria, Lagos. March 1997.

3. Emenuga

"The Nigerian Capital Market and Nigeria's Economic Performance". Paper presented at the Seminar organised by the Nigerian Economic Society at the N.I.I.A., Lagos. January 1998.

4. *Vanguard* Newspaper

"The Nigerian Stock Market in the Next Millennium: Challenges Ahead". Column on Stock Market Round Up.

5. Nigerian Vision 2010 Report

Section on Nigerian Capital Market.

Chapter Three

Some Perspectives on the Development of the Capital Market in Nigeria*

Two of the strategies by which the 1998 policy objectives of the federal government were pursued were guided privatisation of government-owned enterprises and economic liberalisation. Guided privatisation, as it was stated in that budget was a carefully planned and systematically implemented programme of state withdrawal from control of business enterprises which could be more effectively and efficiently run by private operators. It was in the spirit of liberalising the economy that the reorganisation of capital market was pursued to create an enabling environment for both local and foreign investors. The proposal to establish the Abuja Stock Exchange was a bye-product of that initiative.

This chapter starts with the perspective of the Nigerian Capital Market, drawing extensively on the proceedings of the Vision 2010 Committee set up by the Abacha regime in 1997. It discusses current development in the market, and measures introduced by the two regulatory bodies viz., Securities and Exchange Commission (SEC) and the Nigerian Stock Exchange (NSE) to remove some observed shortcomings. A brief exposition of the reorganisation of the Capital Market as contained in both the Odife Panel Report and the 1998 budget leading to the creation of another Stock Exchange, follows ahead. Finally, the chapter examines the pros and cons of a second Stock Exchange in Nigeria.

Paper Presented at a Workshop Organised by Ijewere & Co, held in June, 2000.

Historical Perspective of the Nigerian Capital Market

Before independence, Nigeria lacked an organised Capital Market as we have it today. Despite this handicap, four issues, two government and two industrial loans, were recorded.

Following the recommendation of Barback Committee in 1959, the first attempt at establishing an organised Capital Market began on September 15, 1960, with the incorporation of the Lagos Stock Exchange, through the joint effort of the Central Bank of Nigeria (CBN), Investment Company of Nigeria (later NIDB) and the Nigerian Business Community. Later, the exchange was statutorily empowered in 1961 by the enactment of the Lagos Stock Exchange Act. The Exchange commenced operation on July 5, 1961 with thirteen securities. During the teething stage, the Exchange received considerable financial and other assistance from government through the institutions referred to above.

Some major events occurred in 1962 which had salutary effects on the development of the infant market. These included, the recall of Nigerian investments from London by Nigerian Produce Marketing Company (NPMC), the promulgation of the Exchange Control Act 1962, and the establishment of the Capital Issues Committee (CIC) under the auspices of the Central Bank of Nigeria. Though without any legal backing, the CIC operated like an ad hoc consultative body to ensure the orderly development of the market by regulating share prices and timing of public issues of securities so as not to overtax the absorptive capacity of the budding capital market.

Despite these efforts, activities in the market were generally assessed to be low in the twelve years between 1967 and 1971, as the market was little known by the populace. Government remained a dominant key player especially in the new issues market by regularly floating development loan stocks as a way of stimulating the market. As at the end of 1971, government had floated 39 securities compared to 13 equities and 8 industrial loan stocks. Similarly, the market was characterised by few operators (10), no quoted indigenous company and poor infrastructural facilities.

However, government action in enacting the first Nigerian Enterprises Promotion Act (NEPA) in 1972, which obliged specified alien enterprises to indigenise part of their ownership, made a remarkably positive impact on the development of the market. Within three years of its enactment, twenty new companies were listed on the Exchange, compared to thirteen in twelve years (1960-1971). Again, following the report of the panel set up in 1975 to review the 1972 indigenisation exercise, the second Act was enacted in 1977, ostensibly to correct the "failures" of the first exercise. The rejuvenated 1977 Act brought more companies into the market and consequently, more listings were recorded on the Exchange in years subsequent to its introduction; thus deepening the market. At the height of its compliance in 1979, 39 new companies were listed on the Exchange in that year alone.

Apart from the indigenisation programmes and government's deliberate floating of stocks, four other Government initiatives impacted positively on the development of the capital market as we have it today. These were:

(i)   Enactment of the capital Issues Commission Act in 1973 which formally established the Capital Issues Commission (CIC) and introduced statutory regulation into the market. The functions were not in any way different from that of the defunct committee. For example, it continued the functions of determination of the price, amount, and time at which public issues of corporate securities were made.

(ii)   On April 5, 1976, the Okigbo Committee was set up to undertake a comprehensive review of the Nigerian financial system. With respect to the capital market, the committee made a number of recommendations, many of which were wholly or partially accepted. Amongst these were: establishment of the Securities and Exchange Commission

(SEC), to replace the Capital Issues Commission. Consequently, the Securities and Exchange Commission Act was enacted in 1979. The Act made SEC the apex regulatory institution in the Capital Market in Nigeria. In addition to taking over the functions of the Capital Issues Commission, it was empowered to register securities, operators, stock exchanges and maintain surveillance over the market to prevent abuses and practices that may be detrimental to the orderly development of the Capital Market in Nigeria. In 1988, its functions were enlarged to include approval and regulation of mergers and acquisitions and other forms of business combinations.

The government accepted the need for the Stock Exchange to spread out, it however rejected the use of independent Regional Exchange to achieve this objective. Rather, government established the Nigerian Stock Exchange with trading floors in Lagos, Kaduna, and Port-Harcourt. In mid-1980's, three additional trading floors, Kano, Ibadan and Onitsha were added.

Okigbo Panel also recommended a new secondary pricing system for Government stocks to make them reflect the maturity and yield of the instrument. Hitherto, it was priced at par, making them quite unattractive to investors.

(iii) The Structural Adjustment Programme (SAP) was launched in 1986 to redress serious macro-economic problems. The programme included the rationalisation of the public sector through divestment of government holdings and debt conversion programme. Consequently, government commenced privatisation of its interests in some public companies, some of which were effected through Offer for Sale. The sale of these shares to the investing public further increased the number of tradable securities in the market and thus improved market depth.

(iv)   About the time SAP was launched, the Second-tier Securities Market (SSM) was introduced to attract smaller companies to the market which hitherto could not meet the more stringent listing conditions of the First-tier Market.

The number of tradable securities increased as a result of implementing SAP, with much wider impact on the development of the capital market. In the post-SAP era, the market became a truly capitalist instrument for mobilising and allocating capital funds in the process of wealth creation rather than as a vehicle for wealth distribution, as the pre-SAP activities tended to portray. Policies and strategies tended to be more market related than before. For example, the pricing function hitherto performed by SEC was transferred to market operators (Issuing Houses for new issues and stockbrokers for existing issues.) In addition, the deregulation of the foreign exchange and interest rates, which were the pillars of SAP, encouraged many companies to seek for cheaper source of long-term funds which only the capital market could provide. Thus in the late 80s, there was a spate of rights issues in the market which further increased the market depth.

Recent Developments and Assessment Criteria

The 90s witnessed continued efforts to widen, deepen and improve trading conditions in the Nigerian Stock Market. For example, the Unit Trust Scheme was launched in 1990 as a way to bring small investors indirectly to participate in the fortunes of the Market. The period equally recorded a significant increase in the number of Market Operators (Stockbrokers). The Stock Exchange launched the Central Securities Clearing System (CSCS) in 1997 to usher in a more efficient securities settlement system. As a result of this innovation, settlement of trade also improved from T+14 or more, in some cases in the past, to T + 5. The NSE also introduced Automated Trading System (ATS) in 1988. Tables 3.1 and 3.2 compared the performance of the Nigerian Capital Market between 1961 and 1999 and the last six years.

Table 3.1 provides a snapshot of the 10-year interval up to 1999 and Table 3. 2 illustrates the performance in the last eight years.

Table 3.1 NSE's Growth Trends 1961 – 1999

Parameter	1961	1971	1981	1991	1999
No. of Quoted Companies	3	13	93	142	195
No. of Listed Securities	13	60	163	239	269
Total Mkt. Capitalisation (Billion ₦)	Na	Na	5.0	23.1	263.3
Vol. Of Securities traded (M)	334	952	Na	47.2	216
Value of Securities Traded (MMN)	2.3	18.1	332.1	265	136.3
Value of new shares (MMN)	Na.	87	455	1870	3,954
NSE All Shares Index	Na	Na	Na	783	5266
No. of Stockbroking Firms	Na	Na	12	110	226

Note: End of Period Data

Source: Nigerian Stock Exchange, SEC, FOS.

Table 3.2 NSE's Eight Year Performance Summary

Parameter	1992	1993	1994	1995	1996	1997	1998	1999
No. of Quoted Coys.	153	174	177	181	183	184	186	195
No. of Listed Securities	251	272	276	276	276	267	264	269
Total Mkt. Capitalisation (Billion ₦)	31	47	66	180	286	282	263	300
Vol. of Shares Traded (M)	262	473	524	397	882	557	2,097	3,954
Daily Avg. Vol. of Shares (MM)	1.1	1.9	2.1	1.6	3.5	6.9	8.4	15.6
Price/Earning Ratio	9.0	8.4	5.5	9.2	12.2	14.5	11.9	12
Value of New Issues (Billion ₦)	3.3	2.6	2.2	4.4	21.5	0.6	7.16	1.26
NSE All Shares Index	1108	1544	2205	5092	6992	6441	5673	5266
No. of Stock-broking Firms	140	140	140	162	162	162	186	226

Note: End of Period Data
Source: NSE's Fact Book

A principal component of Nigeria's Capital Market is the Stock Market (Exchange) where equity and debt instruments are the principal means of mobilising and allocating long-term funds. The Nigerian Stock Market has existed for 40 years. Table 3.2 has shown that there are only 184 listed companies on the Exchange as at December, 1999. This translates to about five listings per annum, whereas there are over 200,000 incorporated companies in Nigeria as of same date. The importance of the Capital Market as a source of finance for gross fixed capital formation has been declining since 1992 as shown on Table 3.2. This record is not encouraging. Yet, the need for long-term capital today is no less critical than in the past.

A further assessment of the Nigerian Capital Market can be based on the following indices:

Organisation

(a) Nigerian Stock Exchange has trading floors in Lagos, Kaduna, Port-Harcourt, Kano, Onitsha, Ibadan, and Abuja.

(b) Trades in 262 listed securities as of 31st September 1999 made up of 188 equities, 55 industrial loan (Debenture/Preference) stocks and 19 Government stocks, with a market capitalisation of about ₦287 billion as at August, 31st 1999.

Operational Characteristics

(a) Trading used to be by manual Call-Over System until 1998.

(b) 5% price fluctuation band per trading day.

(c) Brokers allowed to make cross-deal even on large orders.

(d) Prices are market determined by operators.

(e) Settlement is by electronic fund transfer through Central Securities Clearing System (CSCS).

(f) Delivery, typically T+5, i.e 5 trading days after transaction/trading date, now T+3.

(g) Depository used to be physical, but now computerised.

(h) Transaction trading costs: Fixed, but graduated brokers' commission, 1% SEC fee.

(i) New issues cost averaging 10-15% of the proceeds with a lead time averaging six months.

Regulatory Framework

(a) Strong statutory regulation with Securities and Exchange Commission as the apex regulatory institution.

(b) The Nigerian Stock Exchange conducts self-regulation of market activities.

(c) All market activities are guided by extensive securities and investment laws which include: Lagos Stock Exchange Act 1961, Companies and Allied Matters Decree 1990, Trustee Investment Act 1957 & 1962, Insurance Decree of 1990, Investment Promotion Commission Decree 1995, Foreign Exchange (Monitoring and Miscellaneous Decree 1995), etc.

Other Features

(a) Strictly enforces rules, regulations and conduct, to protect investors.

(b) Operates Investor Protection Fund, currently worth 120+million Naira.

(c) Minimal foreign capital inflows; $1.1 million and $32. 9 million in 1995 and 1996 respectively.

(d) Cumbersome and unacceptable procedure for managing foreign portfolio investment flows. Situation has improved by the promulgation of Decree 16 & 17 of 1995.

(e) Information dissemination through computer networks; CAPNET and Reuters Electronic Contributor System and the mass media (TV and Newspapers).

Reorganisation of the Capital Market

In 1998 Government decided to repeal all laws inhibiting competition. As a result, a Legal Committee was set up to identify such laws. Twelve of such laws were identified for amendment and/or abrogation, including laws governing the Capital Market. It was in the spirit of liberalising the economy that machinery was set in motion to reform, modernise and internationalise the Nigerian Capital Market and make it more responsive to the demands and challenges of the new millennium. Arising from these measures, the Abuja Stock Exchange was floated in 1998. The Central Bank of Nigeria (CBN), National Insurance Corporation of Nigeria (NICON), Nigerian Deposit Insurance Corporation (NDIC), and other interested private sector organisations were advised by Government to take steps to implement the decision. Before that time, a panel with Dennis Odife as Chairman, was set up to review the Nigerian Capital Market. Although neither the report of the panel, nor the Government White Paper has been released, some aspects of the report that have become public knowledge are set below:

(i)   proposal to set up a new Stock Exchange and rename the current Stock Exchange.

(ii)   issues of Administration and Governance of the Stock Exchange in particular and the Capital Market in general; and

(iii)   The urgent need to achieve rapid growth in virtually every dimension of the Capital Market (number of securities, volumes and value issued and traded etc.).

There have been reactions from several stakeholders in the capital market against the establishment of a second Stock Exchange. There were very strong opposition to the renaming and re-designation of the Nigerian Stock Exchange as The Lagos Stock Exchange. Fear was also expressed in some quarters that a Government-sponsored new Stock Exchange might have undue advantages over any other competing exchange. Such fear might have influenced government's decision to name the new Stock Exchange "Abuja Stock Exchange" instead of the "Stock Exchange of Nigeria" proposed by Odife Panel. Moreover, few interested private sector organisations and Government Agencies have been advised to set machinery in motion to form the new Stock Exchange, instead of a direct government involvement.

The Case For Another Stock Exchange

It is not uncommon to have more than one Stock Exchange in a country. The U.S.A., Hong Kong, South Africa and India are examples of countries with multiple Stock Exchange. Perhaps the justification for the second Exchange in Nigeria after thirty nine years of existence of a dominant national Stock Exchange, is a fallout from the efforts of Government to remove all laws inhibiting competition. If Government, in its wisdom, has decided to open up all sectors of the economy for private investments to promote competition and efficiency in the system, there is no reason why the capital market should be an exemption. Moreover, concerns have been expressed in some quarters about the adequacy of the structure of the existing Nigerian Stock Exchange (NSE), and its branches in the context of the Federal Government's privatisation programme and the policy of encouraging widespread shareholding.

There are fears in certain sections that Government's participation in the new Stock Exchange will have a distortionary effect on the competitive environment both in terms of favouring the new Exchange against any other, and with regard to the potential for inefficiency in the running of the institution – as has been evident in other essentially private-sector entities which Government has dabbled into. The downgrading of the current Exchange could also have major negative effects on its operation as its standing and status would be subject to speculation at a time when the economy in general needs maximum confidence of local and foreign investors.

Moreover, the apparent needs for the existing Stock Exchange and its system are major issues that need to be addressed which will not be resolved by the advent of a new Stock Exchange, along the lines being advocated. In fact, one of the gaps in the Secondary Market system that needs urgent plugging is the absence of a forum for formalised trading in the securities of unquoted public companies. This is why the major reasons for the proposed Over-The-Counter Market (OTC) are to protect investors by providing a formal, orderly and transparent system for trading in the securities of unquoted public companies and also facilitate compliance with the law which requires that securities of public companies can only be traded by SEC – registered brokers/dealers.

Conclusion

The merits of multiple Stock Exchanges and the promise they hold will be put to test when the Abuja Stock Exchange commences operations. The success of this new effort rests squarely on market Operators and the Government. A market structure practice that sustains and deepens public confidence, and ensures its growth must be pursued. These are the challenges of the proposed reforms. Government on its part should ensure the continued enhancement of the economic structure (infrastructure as well as the super-structure) and regulations to support stability, growth, transparency and accountability. Multiple Stock Exchanges on their own will not create a vibrant and growing capital market. On the other hand, the practitioners, the regulators and government have a great role to play.

Chapter Four

The Impact of the Central Securities Clearing System (CSCS) Operations on the Development of Capital Market in Nigeria

Introduction

The mission statement of the Central Securities Clearing System (CSCS) Limited (The Clearing House) is as follows:

> Our mission is to implement and operate a clearing, depository, settlement and registry system of stock transactions that is efficient, investor-friendly and effective with minimum risk. By extension improved market liquidity, integrity, transparency and attraction for domestic and foreign investors would have been assured.

We can therefore measure the performance of the Clearing House against its mission statement described above. The commencement of CSCS operations on Monday 14th April, 1997 and the Automated Trading System (ATS) that followed it in the late 1999 marked the end of the primitive era of call-over system. Nigeria has thus joined the league of fully computerised capital markets of the world. The ultimate is remote trading where stockbrokers can trade from their various offices. It must be mentioned however, that in spite of the enormous advantages of the new system it has elicited anxiety in some investors who still believe in holding their share certificates. There was even stiff opposition by some pressure groups against the introduction of the

CSCS because of the fear that the new system would be fraught with fraud, lacking in transparency. Events have proved such people wrong as the CSCS has worked very efficiently since its inception in 1997. It will however be naïve to say that there were no initial problems; but such problems have been overcome over time. Increasing confidence is being placed on the system as more and more investors now prefer to put their shareholdings into the clearing system, ostensibly for ease of trading. In order to build greater confidence into the system the relationship between the investor and his stockbroker cannot be over-emphasised. The stockbroker must know his client very well because greater reliance and trust will be placed on the decisions he takes on behalf of the client

Weaknesses Observed in the Capital Market Prior to the Introduction of the CSCS

In order to appreciate the impact of the CSCS on the development of the Nigerian Capital Market, it may be pertinent to highlight some of the weaknesses of the old call-over system:

(a) When shares had been purchased on the floor of the Nigerian Stock Exchange (The NSE) it used to take between three to twelve months before share certificates were received by the buyers from the Registrars.

(b) There used to be cancellation and frequent issuance and re-insurance of share certificates when shares changed hands. That process was very cumbersome, time wasting and expensive, in terms of stationeries.

(c) Every time a shareholder wanted to dispose his shareholding, he would have to submit the share certificate for verification which usually took a long time and thus prevented the selling shareholder from taking quick advantage of capital gains.

(d) Some stockbrokers used to sell what they did not have, while some bought without money to pay hence there were many complaints of failed transaction.

(e) Some shareholders lost their share certificates either through misplacement, wrong addresses, fire hazards, and in some cases, the certificates might be stolen even by relations of the owner.

(f) Other weaknesses of the old system include undue delay, manual operation, manipulation cycle, minimal transparency and other risk factors.

Functions of the CSCS

The functions of the CSCS are no doubt meant to confirm the benefits of the new system as they are meant to obviate the weaknesses of the old system as stated above.

The CSCS was set up to provide central depository for share certificates of companies quoted on The Nigerian Stock Exchange and serves as sub-registry for all quoted securities in conjunction with the Registrars of quoted companies. It also issues Central Securities Identification Numbers to stockbrokers and investors. It undertakes the clearing and settlement of securities transactions. It also provides safe keeping and custodian services in conjunction with custodian members for local and foreign instruments.

Settlement and Custody Operations

In the efforts of CSCS to ensure a dynamic stock market that is responsive to the needs and aspirations of local and foreign investors and considering the peculiar Nigerian environment, they have continued to modify their procedures in consultation with all players in the capital market in order to attain an ideal stock market. Stated below are how it all started and the changes that had to be made in conformity with the dynamics of the stock market.

Method of Processing Certificates at Inception:

At inception, stockbroking firms were licensed by Securities and Exchange Commission (SEC); The Nigerian Stock Exchange (NSE) and eligible with Central Securities Clearing System (CSCS) Limited, were required to submit the following documents at the depository window:

(a)   Share Certificates

The share certificates must be from a quoted company listed with the NSE, acknowledged and authenticated by the company registrars through verification of shareholders signatures.

(b)   Transfer Form

The Transfer Form, which is usually attached to a certificate before verification should be properly completed by the shareholder/transferor and must be verified by the registrar before lodgement. If the verification was witnessed by a stockbroking firm other than the one making the lodgement, the former must endorse the latter.

(c)   CSCS R005 – Shareholders Particulars

This form which should be completed by the investor, contains information about the investor for the account opening requirement in the computer system. The form is expected to be signed by the investor and endorsed by the buying or selling stockbroking firm. The processing of this form enables **Clearing House Number** to be assigned to the new investors to the system.

(d)   CSCS R006 – Certificate Deposit Form (CDF)

The form which was completed and submitted in duplicate at inception, contains columns for the shareholder's name, account number, security code, number of shares and certificate number. It provides the name and code of the stockbroking firm making the lodgement easy to identify. The CDF provides all the data and information on every share certificate being deposited which serves as worksheet for computer input officers.

(e)   CSCS D001 – Deposit Summary Form (DSF)

The total number of all equity certificates being lodged by the stockbroking firm are expected to be indicated in the Equity Box including other shares as the case may be. This form serves as a receipt, which must be stamped and signed by the receiving depository officer in acknowledgement of the lodgement for the day. The receipt must be returned to the depository window the following day in exchange for the approved Certificate Deposit Form for trading by the stockbroking firm. This form was in use at the inception of CSCS and was subsequently discontinued.

Operating Hours

At inception, the Depository opened to stockbrokers for lodgement of securities between 9.00 a.m. – 2.00 p.m. and later adjusted to 7.30 a.m. – 2.00 p.m. for registrars who took over the lodgment of securities from stockbrokers to prevent forgery of registrars signatures.

As soon as lodgement and documentation are concluded, the certificates undergo other stages of processing before data entry into the computer system. This is followed by auditing, dematerialisation, and storing the processed certificates in CSCS vault. After nine months, it was agreed by operators that processed certificates should henceforth be forwarded to the registrars.

First Day of Operation

The CSCS was originally located on the 9th floor of The Exchange House but had to be relocated to the first floor of the same building as a result of the construction of a vault to meet international standards and also enough space for operations.

On the first day of operation, only three stockbroking firms had the courage to make their maiden lodgement as follows:

Stockbroking Firm	No. of Certificates lodged
(a) Prominent Securities Ltd	81
(b) CSL Securities Ltd	14
(c) Falcon Securities Ltd	<u>11</u>
Total certificates lodged	<u>106</u>

These were followed by lodgment from nine stockbroking firms the following day. There was steady increase in lodgment of certificates as the stockbrokers acquired confidence in the new system. The lodgments were processed within 24 hours as expected but some of the approval slips were not ready for collection before trading commenced at 11.00 a.m. the following day because of the continued increase in lodgment of certificates. The procedure, which required only one signatory to sign approval slips, was modified by empowering other senior officers to sign the approval slips in time for them to be placed in their respective boxes before trading.

Modification of Certificate Deposit Form (CDF) – R006

When malpractices by few unscrupulous persons were detected, it became mandatory for the CDF to have a declaration that brokers have the mandate of their client(s) to make certificate lodgement and for them to indemnify CSCS Ltd, of any liability in case of any misrepresentation in the documentation. The CDF must be signed by an accredited representative and the managing director of the stockbroking firm.

Modification of Lodgment Procedure

In order to eliminate the incidence of fraudulent practices in the stock market, it was agreed at a meeting of NSE/CSCS with stockbroking firms and registrars of quoted companies on September 1, 1998, that stockbroking firms should submit their clients' certificates to the registrars with completed transfer forms for verification and four copies of CSCS Certificate Deposit Form for lodgement. The registrars were required to lodge the share certificates with CSCS on behalf of the stockbroking firms after verification. The CSCS therefore discontinued receiving verified share certificates directly from stockbroking firms from November 2, 1998. The registrars now deposit the verified share certificates in batches of securities with schedules that contain the items being lodged, signed by authorised signatories.

Modification of Documentation

As a result of the new certificate lodgement procedure by the registrars on behalf of stockbroking firms, efforts were made to reduce documentation. In effect, Form D001 was discontinued, while Form R005 was de-emphasised. In their places, the Transfer Form became a source of new shareholder's information for account creation in the system.

The stockbroking firms are expected to submit the share certificates with four copies of Certificate Deposit Form and a Transfer Form to cover each batch to the registrars for verification. The registrars are expected to forward batches of verified share certificates to be lodged with CSCS Ltd., security by security with a covering letter containing schedule(s) of the items for acknowledgement and processing with two copies of the certificate deposit form.

Modification of Procedure for Dematerialised Certificates

Over 229,529 share certificates were received into the vault, within 9 months of operation, and at an average rate of 1,300 certificates per day at the time, the vault was almost filled thereby creating space problem.

Consequently, at a meeting held by the operators of the stock market in late 1997, it was agreed that dematerialised share certificates (i.e. certificates already processed in CSCS) should be packaged and sent back to the registrars for their retention within 48 hours of processing. Before the implementation of the newly agreed procedure, it was necessary to audit the over 229,529 processed certificates in CSCS vault. This called for special duty by the entire staff (working extra hours including Sundays) with some added temporary staff known as "task force" to help audit, dematerialize, punch, batch and package the processed certificates, security by security, for each month for dispatch to the various registrars with printout and forwarding letters for their records. It took about three months to clear the backlog before the commencement of the daily audit of day-to-day transactions by the injection of additional staff to implement the arduous task. Certificates received on a particular day are processed on that day, audited with the computer printout the following day to ensure correctness of the information provided in the system before they are dematerialised and sent back to the registrars.

Shift System

As the volume of certificates lodgement increased considerably, it became necessary to increase the staff strength and office equipment vis-a-vis the volume of work in order to meet the targeted 24-hour processing period.

Consequently, shift duty was introduced in May 1997 and staff were placed on three shifts to resume duty as follows:

(a)   7.00 a.m. – 3.00 p.m.

(b)   2.00 p.m. – 9.00 p.m.

(c)   8.00 p.m. – 7.00 a.m.

Each shift is headed by a supervisor and the arrangement has been in force to date.

Procedure for Processing Share Certificates

The share certificates lodged in CSCS go through seven major stages of processing namely, receiving, checking, posting, approving, collating, auditing and dispatching.

The certificates lodged by the representatives of the registrars' departments are received by officers who acknowledge receipt after ensuring that the lodgements correspond with the schedules presented. The lodgements are recorded daily to ascertain the volume received.

The received certificates are moved to the checking officers who ensure that the information on the Certificate Deposit Forms (which serve as worksheet for input officers) correspond with those on the physical certificates.

The approving officers take over the posted items using the physical certificates to approve the posted data/information in the system. These certificates enable the approving officers to detect discrepancies for possible amendments. The approved certificates are then separated from the CDF and arranged, security by security, for the purpose of audit. A copy of the approved CDF is dropped in the box of each of the various stockbroking firms within 24 hours while the CSCS copies are arranged for filing in the file of the various stockbroking firms for future reference.

The audit officers receive printout of all approved items the following day for their audit with the physical certificates in order to detect any possible error for correction.

The three major levels of checks in processing are in place to reduce to the barest minimum or possibly eliminate errors in stock data/ information stored in the electronic system.

The audited certificates are dematerialized and batched, security by security, for dispatch to the registrars. These are accompanied by CSCS forwarding letters which are prepared and batched with the dematerialized certificates for the registrar.

The cycle of processing is usually completed when the dematerialized certificates are ready for dispatch to the registrars.

Trade Allotment

At the commencement of CSCS Ltd., as the clearing, settlement and depository agency for the capital market, trading on the floors of The NSE was by outcry/call-over system. Succinctly put, trading was manual while the clearing and settlement were automated.

Trading Process at the Commencement of CSCS

- There was a call-over chairman that regulated the entire trading activities

- Offers and bids were made in the name of the stockbroking firm and not in the name(s) of the actual transferors and transferees.

- At the end of trading, The NSE back-office produced trading statements for their members. The same reports were given to CSCS in a text format on diskette.

- Trade transactions were transferred into the Depository via the diskette obtained from The NSE on a daily basis.

- Since CSCS maintains shareholders register, details of the sellers and buyers are required for trade transactions clearing and settlement.

- The required trade transaction details were supplied by respective stockbroking firms via allotment forms.

Allotment Procedure

While the use of call-over system of trading lasts, each stockbroking firm is expected to advise the CSCS on the day's transaction within 48 hours via allotment forms.

Database record must exist for all clients contained in the allotment form before it can be processed, otherwise shareholders particulars are attached with the allotment form.

Allotment Form "Offer" – CSCS D002

This form is meant for the selling client only. The stockbroking firm would indicate account number, shareholder's name, security/symbol and the quantity of stocks to be debited from each client's stock account. Without the offer form, it would be impossible for CSCS to know the transferor and the quantity to be transferred.

Allotment Form "Offer" – Example

Member Code: ....
Trade Date: ....
Allotment Date: ....

Shareholder's A/c No.
Name
Security
Qty

4567011
Okon Gabriel
Dunlop
300

The above instruction, which should be duly signed by the authorised representative(s) one of whom should be the managing director, mandates CSCS to debit account number 4567011 belonging to Okon Gabriel with 300 units of Dunlop.

Allotment Form 'Buy' – CSCS D003

The 'Buy allotment form' is for the buying client only. Indications are made of the client's Account Number and name. Also, security/symbol and quantity bought are stated on the allotment form.

Allotment Form "Buy"

Member Code: ....

Trade Date: ....

Allotment Date: ....

Shareholder's A/c No.
Name
Security
Qty

843400
Ahmed Jubril
Dunlop
300

1326041
Ojo Bukky
Dunlop
200

The above allotment Form "Buy" which should be duly signed by the authorised representative(s) instructs CSCS to credit Ahmed Jubril of stock account number 843400 with 300 units of Dunlop and Ojo Bukky of Account number 1326041 with 200 units of Dunlop.

For a Deal Involving Two Stockbroking Firms – (Inter-Broker deal)

Allotment form offer and/or Buy were filled depending on the part of the transaction of the stockbroking firm. The stockbroking firm that offered the stock would fill only the allotment offer whereas the stockbroking firm that bought the stock would fill only the allotment Buy and forward same to CSCS for necessary action.

The following rules were put in place to ensure accuracy and timeliness of information supplied:

* The allotment forms, offer and Buy, were to be submitted within 48 hours after trading.

* Stockbrokers were expected to cross-check allotment forms before submitting same to CSCS.

    Client's account number from, say stockbroking firm 'A', must not be used or referenced by another stockbroking firm.

* The trading statement from the Back Office of The Exchange was a very important document that aided brokers in the allotments of shares. This was because only what is recorded at the back office of The Exchange is seen in the CSCS system as having been traded. So, stockbrokers were advised to go through the trading statement and use same while filling the allotment forms. In the event of any disparity between what is traded and the units recorded, stockbrokers should notify the Back Office of The Exchange immediately for verification and correction where necessary.

* For a stockbroking firm to sell stocks of a client that has inventory with another stockbroking firm, an inter-member transfer must first be executed.

Problems Associated with Allotment Form

Common mistakes associated with the content of allotment forms that are filled and submitted by stockbroking firms include:

- Inaccurate client account number
- Wrong security/symbol code
- Aggregate allotted stock units either more or less than traded units
- Inconsistency in the ordering of client names i.e. last name, middle name and first name inconsistency
- Actual traded date different from the one quoted by stockbroking firm
- One allotment form used for more than one trade date.
- Different allotment forms submitted for same date transactions

Account Types

When a new stockbroking firm is registered with CSCS Ltd, four different accounts are opened for the stockbroking firm. The four accounts are:

Traded Stock Account
Deposit Stock Account
Group Account
Client's Account

- The **Traded Stock Account** or Box/House Account was for already traded stocks that were awaiting eventual allotment to clients. Unalloted traded stocks were held in this account. Stocks in the traded stock account were allotted to the client through letters signed by authorised representatives. Stockbroking firms were expected to indicate the client's name, account number, symbol/security to be allotted and the volume. There was no need for allotment form to be filled in this case because the shares were already traded.

- The **Deposit Stock Account** holds the stocks that belong to the house that are yet to be traded. Until the stock in this account is traded, it cannot be allotted to any client. This is unlike Traded stock account. The stocks in the Deposit stock account are not clients' stocks but the stocks in the name of the stockbroking firm.

- **Group Account**. This account is for CSCS in-house use. Before the tight-coupling of the **Equator** (Depository's software package) with the **Horizon** (Automated Trading System, ATS) all the transactions went into this account. It was from here that allotments were made to rightful owners. It must not be referenced at all by the stockbrokers. It keeps track of the actual total volume of stock traded for each stockbroking firm.

- **Client's Account**. This is the account that is system generated via the use of "particulars of shareholder". It is stockbroking firm dependent. The account numbers are unique. The client's shares inventories are logged into this stock account.

Inter-member Transfer

This affords investors freedom of action. Investors are allowed to transfer custody of their investment to any stockbroking firm of choice at any time. Investors are not compelled to do stock transactions perpetually with a stockbroking firm. If a stockbroking firm is sanctioned by the regulatory authorities, clients can transfer custody of their investment to any chosen stockbroking firm.

If Transfer is Initiated by the Resident (current) Firm

Steps:

1. The stockbroking firm would write CSCS to move the client

account (based on the client's request) to another stockbroking firm. This letter would be addressed to the Managing Director/ CEO of CSCS.

2. The letter would state the name of the client, account number, name of stock and quantity of stock to be moved.

3. Confirmation of the transfer from CSCS can be obtained through the acknowledgement copy of the transfer letter.

4. Thereafter, the new house could go ahead to trade on the stock.

If Transfer is Initiated by the Target Stockbroking Firm

The new house would write a letter to CSCS (addressed to the Managing Director/CEO) with client's letter of instruction to the stockbroking firm attached, stating that he wants to transfer his account with the specified stock(s) and quantity from his **former house** to the **new house**.

The **former house** would be copied.

Confirmation of the transfer from CSCS can be obtained through the acknowledgement copy of the transfer letter. Thereafter, the broker would go ahead to trade on the stock(s).

Common Mistakes Associated with Inter-member Transfers:

1. Some stockbroking firms initiating the transfers did not ascertain if the stocks were still available before initiating letters of transfer. This was necessary in order to reduce faulty transfer request.

2. Transfer requests were usually made to the Traded Stock Account of the target stockbroking firm. This was wrong and unacceptable because it amounted to changes of ownership without trades.

3. The Clearing House Number and the Stock Account Number of the clients being transferred in some instances were not stated for ease of transfer.

4. There were open-ended transfer requests such as: "transfer all the stocks belonging to Mr. A". This kind of request could not be treated because the names of the stocks and the quantities to be moved were not explicitly stated.

5. Some shareholders instructed CSCS to transfer their accounts to other houses. Instructions of that nature were expected to come through their stockbroking firms.

6. Letter of consent from the target house without the acknowledgement of the client's former house was not entertained.

Bank Settlement Procedure During T+5 Settlement Cycle

In 1997, when CSCS Ltd., commenced operation, the T+5 settlement cycle was introduced [T+5 implies: Transaction Day plus five working days]. By this rule, the transaction of today will settle by next five working days.

The Procedure is as Follows:

1. Stockbroking firms would fund their Trading Account at a day before the transaction day [Day T - 1].

2. The unblocked balances as at T-1 are considered available **only** for Day T transaction.

3. On daily basis, the financial commitment of each stockbroking firm is blocked by the settlement bank

4. By 9.00 a.m. of every trading date, settlement banks would advise CSCS on the unblocked current balances of each stockbroking firm.

5.   CSCS collates and merges all the bank advice.

6.   CSCS forwards the balances to The Exchange

7.   At the end of trading, The Exchange matches each day's bank balance with each broker's net balance for that day.

8.   A broker's bank balance for the day **must** be sufficient enough to pay for the days transactions. A debit balance/difference is considered as overtrade. Such identified over-trades are cancelled by The Exchange.

9.   The Exchange forwards to CSCS clean and certified transactions for the day

10.   CSCS processes same and sends the day's financial commitment of stockbroking firms to their respective settlement banks on Day T+3.

11.   Settlement banks go for clearing on Day T+4 while payments are made on Day T+5.

Processing of Branch Trades:

Transactions from The Exchange branches were accorded the same treatment as those from the Head Office in Lagos. The steps followed were:

•   Trades for the day were compiled by the branch manager and forwarded to the Head Office.

•   The dated receipt at the Head Office was taken as the systems transaction date. Note that transactions could not be back-dated or post-dated.

•   The branch trades were merged with the Head Office trades. The merged transactions were forwarded to CSCS for clearing and settlement.

•   While floor transactions were forwarded to The Exchange by the branch manager, allotment forms for the stock allocation were sent to CSCS by the stockbroking firms individually. The branch venue was supposed to be highlighted on the "Allotment form". The following problems were identified:

- Allotment forms got to the CSCS after settlement of the transactions.

- Allotment forms were usually received without matching floor transactions and vice versa.

- Conflicting system transaction, date and actual transaction date.

- To facilitate processing before settlement date, fax copies sent were blurred.

Joint action was taken by The Exchange and the CSCS to address these problems. A committee was set up to implement agreed procedure.

- All mails meant for The Exchange and CSCS to be collated by the branch manager. The mails include floor transactions and brokers allotment forms, transferee's transfer forms, letters etc.

- The NSE paid for the items to be couriered.

- Designated officers receive and treat the items with dispatch.

- Acknowledgement/treated copies of items and other mails sent to destination through the established courier system.

CSCS-Registrar Data Update:

The CSCS on weekly and bi-weekly basis, (depending on the size and activity level of the register) updates the registers of quoted companies on transactions that took place on all the floors of The Nigerian Stock Exchange, through diskettes and hard copies. The update contains list of certificates deposited within the period of advice, the master file which contains names, clearing house numbers and activities of investors and the transaction file which contains transactions that took place within the period of advice. Registrars are expected to update their registers promptly.

It is pertinent to state that the CSCS-Registrar data update operated on monthly basis at the commencement of CSCS for all quoted securities. The format, frequency of update and other issues were agreed to at the committee of stakeholders before the CSCS started operation.

Introduction of Pre-Trading Form (PTF)

Owing to the problems of short selling associated with the allotment offer procedure, CSCS came up with Pre-Trading Account on October 2nd 1998. This was to further ensure that trades would not fail; that stockbrokers could not sell what was not available, and to afford capacity/ability of determining stocks on **offer.**

Under the procedure, stockbroking firms were expected to advise the CSCS at least 24 hours before the trade date on all the shares they had mandate to sell using "PTF – Offer" form. The following is a specimen of PTF offer form. The form was to be stamped and signed by authorized representatives.

PTF Offer

Member Code: ....

Date: ....

Shareholder's A/c No.
Name
Security
Qty

148690
Ebun Jack
Agip
400

The above PTF Offer form instructs the CSCS to debit the shareholder's account number 148690 with 400 units of AGIP Plc and credit the Pre-Trading Account of the stockbroking firm. The Pre-Trading Account is the Deposit Account that holds stocks to be traded. The Allotment Offer form was discontinued. The Buy Allotment form/ Transferees form was still relevant, and the process continued until February 28, 2000 when the Automated Trading System (Horizon) of The Exchange was tightly coupled with that of the CSCS-CSD (The Equator). The brokers were thereafter expected to sell and buy directly from and to clients' accounts electronically. Hence, the PTF and Allotment form Buy were discontinued.

Post ATS Procedure

The introduction of Automated Trading System has put an end to the Call-Over system of stock trading. Instead of the shouting on the floor to announce intention to sell or buy securities, the brokers interact with one another through inter-connected work stations across the network.

This evolution which gave dynamism to the capital market involves the broker interacting with the system online, real time. Under this method, the stockbrokers no longer advise CSCS through allotment forms after trade; rather, they input interactively, the account numbers of the seller/buyer of the security and the quantity of stocks. The system receives the inputed data, queries the CSCS database to match the inputed data with the data in CSCS client's database to confirm the existence of inventory in the transferor's account and the existence of the transferee. This is done before allowing the transaction, otherwise the transaction is rejected.

The CSD Software Package [Equator]

The CSCS (Equator) is made up of a set of closely integrated but separate modules that can be configured through parameters to support a broad set of security instruments, risk models and settlement cycles.

The equator is functionally rich, highly scalable, flexible, secure and integrated to provide true Straight Through Processing and ensure delivery versus payment. The Equator's six (6) integrated modules support any environment and a wide variety of securities instruments in different markets. The modules are:

- ˙Depository/Registry with corporate actions support
- Clearance and Settlement
- Administration and Billing
- Pledge Management (Collateral Management)
- Borrowing/Lending and
- Risk Management/Withdrawals

The system is parameter-based hence easily customisable and maintainable. The CSCS (Equator) supports multiple markets with different rules – sets, price discovery mechanisms, listing requirements, transaction type, settlement terms and policies. It supports the following securities instrument through all aspects of depository, clearing, settlement and registry functions:

- Equities
- Rights/Warrants
- Fixed income Instruments
- Commodities
- Derivatives
- Money Market Instruments (T-Bills, etc)
- Electronic Initial Public Offering (EIPO).

The CSCS equator supports the underlisted security market environments.

- Certificated
- Immobilised
- Dematerialised
- Combined environments

The CSCS (Equator) Systems support the following:
- International Standards
- G. 30 recommendations
- Listed and unlisted markets
- 9.9 billion Accounts currently
- National Identification Numbers (NIN)
- Regional/Across the Border Identification Numbers
- Delivery Versus Payment
- Real-Time Gross Settlement
- Multilateral Netting (Cash)
- Trade for Trade (Securities)

It also adapts to the unique characteristics and realities of individual markets. The Nigerian Stock Market is an example.

Corporate actions are a reflection of a security's history. CSCS (equator) supports the underlisted corporate action:
- Bonus issues
- Dividends
- Rights/Warrants
- Debentures
- Interest
- Consolidations
- Maturity Payments
- Share Splits
- Mergers/Takeovers
- Repos
- Name Changes/Address Changes
- Portfolio Valuations

The Corporate Action Diary is also available to all participants online. The CSCS (Equator) is designed to support **multiple languages**. For each user, the system administrator can specify the language of choice:

- English
- French
- Arabic
- Japanese

The CSCS (Equator) supports **multiple currencies** within the software. Exchange rates can be set within the software on as needed basis. All changes are logged.

The CSCS (Equator) is fully year 2000 complaint. Calendar rules can be customised to meet regional or local requirements, such as supporting a **Hajre Calendar for Islamic States.**

The CSCS (Equator) application software provides numerous inquiries and reports for the users of the system. These inquiries and reports include:

- General Inquiries
- Member Account List
- Beneficial Owner lists
- Statement of Account Report
- Vault Reconciliation Report
- Auditing Inquiry
- Warnings over Audit Report
- Corporate Actions Diary.

The CSCS system is very versatile. It can function in a decentralised environment, supporting banking environment because it was initially conceived to be a bank.

The NSE's *Horizon* and The CSCS *Equator* have been proven technologically and can be used as stand-alone products or fully integrated towards a Straight-Through Processing (STP) model. The STP model offers the end-to-end automation of the trading process within and between buy and sell supporting institutions, from the first captive of an order through to final settlement.

The CSCS (Equator) started as a stand-alone before it was tightly-coupled with the trading system (ATS) of The NSE.

The CSCS (Equator) can be interfaced to different trading systems, Clearance, Settlement, Depository and Registry Systems, to provide an integrated and complete capital markets solution.

Achievements of the CSCS to Date

1. Transaction cycle reduced from 6 months or more to 4 days (T+3).

2. Inter-Broker Settlement reduced from 14 days to 4 days (T+3).

3. Transparency in the capital market has been enhanced. Investors can make direct enquiry of their shareholdings from CSCS.

4. Registrars of quoted companies are advised weekly and bi-monthly in order to update investors database promptly unlike the pre-CSCS days when it took several months to update investor's account after transaction.

5. Brokers cannot sell what they do not have in CSCS database due to tight coupling with the ATS (Trading Engine).

6. Trade Guarantee Fund (TGF) ensures no failed trades.

7. Lien placement is easily perfected with minimum delay.

8. Stockbrokers can at a glance know their total portfolio through CSCS.

9. The CSCS system can easily identify any stockbroking firm that transacted on stolen certificates to enable their recovery.

10. Shareholders are relieved of keeping bulky number of certificates that represent their stockholdings. They no longer have to wait for years for re-issuance of certificates.

11. The stockholding of shareholders can be displayed on a statement of stock position and seen at a glance.

12. Stocks in the system can be used as collateral with the confirmation of the stockholdings and placing of lien by the CSCS.

13. Verification of certificates has been encouraged to be hastened by the need for automated processing by the registrars.

14. The CSCS system can place caution on missing certificates to enable them to be easily detected when subsequently lodged for processing.

15. If CSCS is informed of any fraudulent lodgment, the stock can be placed on hold to disable its transfer until the matter is resolved.

16. Special Stock Accounts exist for any willing investor who wants to take full control of his/her stockholding in CSCS.

17. No less than 17,054,992,531 shares, originating from 1,553,292 share certificates have been deposited with the CSCS system to date – December 2001. Thus, the shares are ready for immediate trading.

In the Year 2000

•   Cleared and settled 5.2 billion shares worth ₦28.3 billion

•   Of the 600,000 shareholders in CSCS system, only 3,784 shareholders have requested for certificates since inception. For year 2000, only 1900 shareholders requested for certificates

In the Year 2001

•   Phone-In-Service to ascertain holdings in CSCS system

- T+3 settlement cycle
- Cleared and settled 6.01 billion shares worth ₦57.55 billion
- 750 shareholders requested for share certificates.

Operators in the CSCS System

Investors

Investors or shareholders are the pivot of the activities in the capital market. They initiate activities with the mobilisation of funds and securities, which they place at the disposal of their brokers for investment decisions on their behalf.

Stockbroking Firms

Stockbroking firms licenced by SEC and The Exchange mobilise investors to lodge stocks with CSCS for transactions on the floors of The Exchange and funds with the settlement banks for settlement of transactions entered into on their behalf. They are now responsible for the allotment of traded shares in the system since the tight coupling of the ATS and CSCS Server became effective in early 2000.

Registrars/Custodian Services

Stanbic Bank Nigeria Ltd provides custodian services on behalf of its clients. These services include – attending Annual General Meetings, receiving dividend payments and maintaining nominal accounts.

Registrars pay dividend warrants, issue bonuses scrips to shareholders whose names appear on the register on closure date.

The registrars of quoted companies, aside from corporate functions (custodial services) they perform on behalf of their companies, have continued to be relevant in the operations of CSCS. They interface with the CSCS to update the registers of quoted companies with transactions that take place on the floors of The Exchange and they also ensure that investors get benefits for their investment. Their duties called for automation of their procedures to be able to accommodate transactions updates from CSCS. They had to cope with the problems associated with change which resulted in their having to make lodgements with CSCS on behalf of stockbroking firms for the successful implementation of the new system.

The CSCS, on weekly and bi-weekly basis, advises the registrars of quoted companies on transactions that take place on the floors of The Exchange. The advice is both on diskettes and hard copies. The advice relates to particulars of certificates deposited within the period of advice, the master file containing information on investors and the transaction file containing the transactions that took place within that period of advice.

Registrars are expected to update their database with CSCS advice. This is to ensure that at each point in time the current position of an investor's holdings with CSCS is the same with the registrar's CSCS balance at the registrar's office. This is to avoid conflict.

Settlement Banks

The four settlement banks namely Citibank Nigeria (formerly NIB), Citizens International Bank Ltd, Diamond Bank Ltd and FSB International Bank Plc, have been in partnership with CSCS to ensure the success of the T+5 settlement cycle and later the current T+3 settlement cycle.

There is also an interface with CSCS to achieve Delivery Versus Payment (DVP) and the maintenance of the Trading Account of the stockbroking firms. Discussions are currently going on between the banks and CSCS on the operation of T+1 settlement cycle.

Regulatory Authorities

The efforts of the regulatory authorities in the CSCS cannot be over-emphasised. The SEC provided the enabling environment in the licensing of CSCS, provided surveillance and supervisory role while The

Exchange being the parent organisation provided the capital base and also continues to provide the trading environment.

The SEC, The Exchange and CSCS apply persuasion and in some cases disciplinary measures on operators in order to maintain a transparent and vibrant capital market in Nigeria.

CSCS Flow of Activities

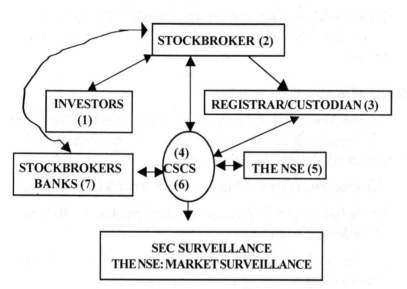

Trading, Clearing and Settlement Process:

The Investor

- The investor initiates any transaction on his investment by approaching a stockbroking firm that is a member of The Nigerian Stock Exchange.

- He is required to deposit his money with the stockbroking firm where he is buying, or deposit his Equity/Debenture certificates for verification where he is selling.

- He completes the necessary documentation – including Transfer Form.

- For a part-seller, he gives instruction to his stockbroking firm to sell from the stocks.

- Where certificates have been dematerialised he gives instruction to his stockbroking firm to sell from the shareholding in the CSCS system.

- Institutional or high net-worth investors are allowed to open special accounts with CSCS to encourage them to invest in the stock market.

The Stockbroking Firm

- The stockbroking firm apart from being licenced by The NSE registered by Securities and Exchange Commission (SEC) is expected to be eligible with CSCS Ltd.

- Nominates two (2) accredited stockbrokers/officials to CSCS.

- Maintains only one Trading Account at any point in time with one of the designated settlement banks.

- Instructs the bank to obey CSCS instruction as it relates to the Trading Account.

- Receives orders/instructions from investors and fills out certificate deposit form in quadruplicate, sends them with certificate(s) to the registrar for verification.

- Verifies clients/investors signatures with the registrars.

- Gives contract notes to investors as evidence of contract.

Registrars in Matters Relating to CSCS

- In matters relating to stock market securities trading, the registrars are to deal only with the stockbroking firms registered with The Exchange, and acting on behalf of investors/shareholders.

- Verifies/authenticates investors claims (i.e. certificates and transfer forms) as presented through the stockbroking firm(s).

- Sends verified certificate(s) and the signed Transfer Form with two (2) copies of certificate deposit form(s) to the depository of CSCS within 48 hours.

The CSCS

- The particulars in the Transfer Form; form the database for opening account and subsequent transactions update to the registrars.

- System generated account number is taken by the CSCS system, but the book-entry will in addition reflect the account number on the lodged certificates;

- CSCS issues Certificate Deposit Form, which certifies that the shares are now in the CSCS system and entitles stockbrokers to trade the shares.

- In effect, all shares to be traded on the floors of The Nigerian Stock Exchange must have their certificates verified by the relevant registrars and recorded in electronic book-entry in the depository of CSCS for the account of the Selling Dealing Member prior to being eligible to be traded.

The Nigerian Stock Exchange

- Provides the venue for trading on capital market securities through licensed stockbrokers

- Checks and validates deals done on daily basis.

- Transmits to CSCS online real time basis through Automated Trading System (ATS) on transactions that occur on the floors of

The Exchange. This is currently available in our website – www.cscs_csd.com

At CSCS

- Transactions obtained from The Exchange are processed

- Stockbrokers daily financial commitment to each other are communicated to the settlement banks via diskettes supported by hard copies.

Settlement Banks

The four banks are well capitalised and have met CBN requirements as follows:

- Settlement banks can only allow Trading Accounts to be operated on the basis of written instructions by either the Dealing Member who maintains the Trading Account or those contained in CSCS schedules.

- Settlement banks can only permit Trading Accounts to be used for purposes of effecting settlement of CSCS transactions.

- The primary mode of settlement of CSCS transactions by settlement banks is by means of Inter-Bank Settlement System (NIBSS). Alternative means provided for are:

(a) Payment by managers cheque (bank draft) and (b) Payment of cash at the counter of the settlement banks.

T+3 Transaction Cycle - Current Procedure
The transaction cycle transited from T+5 at inception, to T+3 on March 1, 2000.

Day T: By 4.00 p.m. of Day T (Transaction Day), CSCS sends advice of Day T stockbroking firms' net financial obligations to their respective settlement banks. This is an information to alert the banks about their clients commitment on Day T+3.

Day T+2: By 12 noon of Day T+2, settlement banks to alert CSCS about the possibility of any broker's inability to meet his financial obligation on Day T+3.

Day T+3: The alert can be by fax, e-mail, letter or telephone or a combination of any two of the above.

Stockbroking firms are to verify from their settlement banks, The Exchange and CSCS, their ability to meet their financial obligation on their Day T transaction on Day T+3.

By 6.00 p.m. of the Day T+2, CSCS sends advice of Day T transactions, stockbroking firms' net financial obligations to their respective settlement banks for processing.

Day T+3 – By 9.00 a.m. stockbroking firms/custodians or any high net-worth individual input have funded their accounts for Day T transactions.

Settlement banks debit and/or credit on Day T+3, stock settlement effected on Day T+3. In effect, Delivery Versus Payment (DVP) is achieved.

Trade Guarantee Fund (TGF)

– Trade Guarantee Fund has been established by stockbroking firms. The CSCS opened Nominee Account in each of the four (4) settlement banks – Diamond Bank of Nigeria Ltd., Citibank Nigeria Ltd. – (formerly NIB), Citizens International Bank Ltd., and FSB International Bank Plc.

– The stockbroking firms contributed ₦50,000 each to the pool at their respective settlement banks or through The Exchange.

– Any overtrading is settled from the Trade Guarantee Fund Account. In general, there is no cancellation of trades any more.

Automation – Automated Trading System (ATS)

– The Nigerian Stock Exchange has upgraded the stock market towards internationalization of its operations by way of automation of the stock market process.

– The call-over system i.e. manual trading system has been replaced by electronic trading by brokers – Automated Trading System (ATS).

– The Nigerian Stock Exchange Automated Trading System (ATS) runs on the horizon trading Software developed by EFA Software Services Limited.

– The next stage of full automation of trading in securities will be for brokers to migrate to their offices and trade remotely with their computers.

Chapter Five

Role of Domestic and International Capital Markets in the Recapitalisation of Banks in Nigeria*

Introduction

This chapter will focus on the roles of domestic and international capital Markets in the recapitalisation of banks in Nigeria.

The Hon. Minister of Finance in his 1997 budget statement explained that the minimum paid-up capital required of banks was last fixed in mid-1991, and therefore needed to be reviewed in the light of depreciating exchange rate, inflation rate trends, and the erosion of the capital funds of banks by non-performing credits, as well as the need to ensure consistency with international standards. The minimum paid-up capital requirement of both commercial and merchant banks was therefore increased to a uniform level of ₦500 million. Existing banks were required to meet the requirement over a transitional period of two years, expiring 31st December, 1998. Banks which failed to meet the requirement by that date would have their licences revoked while new banks are supposed to comply with that condition before they are licensed.

The issue of distressed banks is, no doubt, a major problem plaguing the banking sector in Nigeria in recent years. Some banks have fallen

Paper Presented at a Workshop on Recapitalisation of Banks in Nigeria Organised by the Chartered Institute of Bankers of Nigeria at Bankers House, PC 19, Adeola Hopewell Street, Victoria Island, Lagos, March, 1997.

by the way side as evidenced by the liquidation of four banks in 1994 and the acquisition and subsequent intention to sell, of ten other banks by the Central Bank of Nigeria (CBN). In addition, quite a number of the existing ones are in distress, resulting in the assumption of control of seventeen such banks by the CBN. Consequently, licensed banks have lost some of the confidence which they hitherto enjoyed. The potential negative effects of this problem, if allowed to remain with us for too long, are of such magnitude as to damage the banking system and the economy as a whole.

There is thus the urgent need to deal effectively with the problem. It is in the light of this that government directed that banks should increase their capital base. However, the big leap of an average of 1025% over the present level and the short time stipulated for compliance leave much to be desired.

Recent Basic Financial Information of Nigerian Banks

For the purpose of this chapter, the analysis will be limited to publicly quoted banks and some private banks as follows:

Table 6.1 Basic Financial Information on Some Nigeria Banks

Banks	Authorised Capital ₦	Paid-Up Capital ₦	Ownership Structure
1. Afribank	575m.Ord. 25m Pref.	281.25m Ord.	Nigerians 44% BIAO (now in hand) 40%, Staff 6%
2. First Bank	300m.	215m.	100% Nigerians
3. FSB Int'l	300m	139.135m	Nigerian citizens and Associations – 100%
4. Guaranty Trust	200m	200m	Nigerians – 100%
5. Highland Bank	150m	50m	Nigerians – 100%
6. Inland Bank	400m	200m	Nigerians – 100%
7. IMB	197m. Ord. 3m. Pref.	87m	
8. Lion Bank	100m	60.266m	Nigerians – 100%
9. Mercantile Bank	75m	50m	Nigerian – 100%
10. NAL	100m	94.5m	Nigerian Citizens and Associations – 100%
11. Orient Bank	200m	50m	Nigerians – 100%
12. Omega Bank	285.m	50m	Nigerians – 100%
13. Progress Bank	100m	25m	Nigerians – 100%
14. Savannah Bank	I billion	52.383m	Nigerians – 100%
15. Trade Bank	250m	200m	Nigerians – 100%
16. Trans International	200m	107.25	Nigerians – 100%
17. UBA	300m	300m	Nigerians – 100% Foreign – 40%
18. Union Bank	500m	158.7m	Nigerians – 100%
19. Wema Bank	300m	138m	Nigerians – 100%
20. Chartered Bank	250m	147.169m	Nigerians – 25% Foreign – 75%

21. NIB	500m	500m	Nigerians – 100%
22. Nigeria Inter-Continental	250m	100m	Nigerians – 100%
23. IBTC	150m	100m	Nigerians – 100%
24. Liberty Merchant Bank	100m	100m	Nigerians – 100%
25. Diamond Bank	200m	152m	Nigerians – 100%
26. Citizen	200m	150m	Nigerians – 100%
27. ECO Bank	250m	133.5	Nigerians – 100% Foreign – 40%
28. Zenith	350m	242.83m	Nigerians – 100%
29. Credit Lyonnais	120m	120m	Nigerians – 100% Foreign – 40%
30. Equatorial Trust	500m	250m	Nigerians – 100%

The data provided on Table 6.1.(1997) indicates that only five of the banks have authorised capital of ₦500 million and above, only one bank, Nigeria International Bank (NIB) met the minimum capital requirement of ₦500m, and five banks have a mixed capital structure of both Nigerian and Foreign shareholders. Two banks, Afribank and IMB have a mixture of ordinary and preference shares. Twenty out of the thirty banks considered had anticipated the need to increase their paid-up capital to above ₦100m from the minimum of ₦50m stipulated in 1991, an action considered to be very forward looking and proactive. The corollary is that these forward-looking banks are the ones that have performed better in recent times in terms of turnover and profitability as available data indicates.

The Role of Capital in Efficient Management of the Banking Institution

The fundamental operations of banks from time immemorial has been the acceptance of funds from depositors and to lend same to those with ability to use additional funds for productive purposes. The capacity of banks to successfully perform the above function without the risk of failure depends on the following:

(1) Quality and sustainability of bank earnings;

(2) The sufficiency of liquidity;

(3) The adequacy of capital

In other types of business, levels of operation are essentially determined by the relative size of their capital but in the banking sector this is not necessarily so because of the fundamentals of banking as earlier stated. Thus, banks usually employ very little of their funds in relation to the volume of their operations.

In the drive to acquire profit yielding assets, banks are confronted with a number of risks, some of which are liquidity risk, income risk, market risk, operational risk, ownership/management risk, including foreign exchange risk. In spite of the inherent risks in the banking industry, the responsibilities of the bank to its stakeholders demand that it strives to generate wealth. The inherent risk in the industry, at times do crystalise as financial losses.

In view of the potential to incur losses, banks should maintain a level of capital that is adequate for its level of operations, expansion of its assets base and liabilities. The adequacy of capital provides investors/depositors with a certain level of comfort for the confidence required in the system. It indeed provides the safety net that allows banks to remain solvent and continue operating despite unexpected macro-economic or institutional difficulties. It further enforces discipline in private banks since they must subject themselves to market scrutiny in order to augment their capital base.

Having established the importance of capital in the banking institutions, a fundamental question is, how much capital is adequate for a bank or type of bank? A review of literature indicates this issue has been a topic of debate for years. A number of methods have been proposed, used, and/or discarded. The following approaches have been tried in measuring the capital adequacy of banks:

(1)   **Deposit Based Ratio**
This approach requires deposit takers to maintain a certain level of capital in proportion to their level of deposits.

(2)   **Asset Based Ratio**
This approach views capital as the cushion that makes up the denomination in the real value of assets. The capital adequacy computation in this formula is based on the level of risk-weighted assets or total assets.

(3)   **Bank Committee**
The Bank Committee on Banking Regulations and Supervisory Practices, representing the views of the group of ten Central Banks, recommended a risk weighted capital adequacy of 8 per cent. The Nigerian monetary authority adopted the recommendation in the 1996 Monetary Policy circular which stipulated as follows:

> In keeping with international standards, the minimum ratio of capital to risk-weighted assets shall remain 8.0 per cent in 1996. Furthermore, at least 50 per cent of the components of a bank capital shall comprise paid-up capital and reserves, while every bank maintains a ratio of not less than one to ten (1:10) between its adjusted capital funds and its total credit.

It is noteworthy that different capital requirements obtain in different countries. In Nigeria, unless the policy is changed, one can safely state that all banks irrespective of their asset or deposit base must have a minimum paid-up capital of ₦500 million. Failure to do this means the bank's capital will be adjudged inadequate, with the bank at the risk of losing its operating licence.

Banking Environment and the Financial Condition of Banks

The environment in which banks operate contribute largely to their performance and vice versa. A bank's environment includes the economic, socio-political and the regulatory/supervisory environments. The policy thrust of the 1997 Federal Government Budget which aimed at bringing about further reduction in the rate of inflation, induce a higher rate of output growth and employment, and strengthen the external sector and the naira exchange rate, will no doubt enhance the performance of banks. The policy instruments are all highlighted in the Budget Statement of the Hon. Minister of Finance. On the political front, it is gratifying to note that democracy which Nigeria is enjoying at present is a condition precedent to economic growth.

The financial condition of many of the banks is very precarious. Many of them are grossly under-capitalised for their levels of operation. The under-capitalisation is largely due to the amount of non-performing loans which had eroded the capital base of many banks. Capital adequacy therefore, as measured by the ratio of loans and advances to shareholders' funds, is very deficient. It is therefore appropriate for government to direct that all banks should increase their paid-up capital to a minimum of ₦500m.

Capital Market

A brief review of the nature of the capital market is a prerequisite to our discussion on the role of both the domestic and international capital markets in the recapitalisation of Nigerian Banks.

Capital markets exist to provide long-term capital to government and corporate bodies, for industrial and socio-economic as well as infrastructure development purposes. The capital market deals with financing instruments of long-term nature. These instruments include equities (ordinary shares) and bonds. The Capital Market may be differentiated from the money market in terms of the maturity profile of the instruments issued and traded. The money market essentially consists of short-tenured instruments, often of less than one year maturity, such as Bankers Acceptance, Commercial Papers and Treasury Bills.

Domestic Capital Market

By certain measures, the Nigerian Capital Market is one of the most developed and attractive on the African continent and compares favourably with some emerging markets outside the region. The country has one stock exchange – The Nigerian Stock Exchange with headquarters in Lagos and branches in Ibadan, Kaduna, Kano, Port Harcourt and Onitsha; established over three decades ago as a private company limited by guarantee. As at mid-August 1996, the Exchange had on its trading board 274 securities, of which 183 were equity listings, covering virtually every sector of the economy, from manufacturing to aviation. The market also prides itself with some of the most reputable and profitable companies in the country having strong links or subsidiary relationship with well known multinational corporations.

The number of quoted companies on the Nigerian Exchange (181 at the end of 1995) surpassed equity listings on emerging markets such as Portugal (169), Poland (65), Jordan (97), Russia (170), Argentina (149) and Venezuela (90), and on mature markets like Austria (109), Belgium (143), Norway (151) and Finland (73). It was higher than all markets in Africa with the exception of South Africa and Egypt. The point is that the Nigerian Capital Market provides greater options to investors in terms of choice of equities than most other African Markets do. Ghana for instance, had only 19 companies listed, Botswana 12, Kenya 56, Tunisia 26, Cote d' Ivoire 31, and Zimbabwe 64 in 1995. The growth of equity listing on the Nigerian Stock Exchange in the 1990s is primarily a factor of the privatisation exercise of the Federal Government which brought 28 new companies to The Exchange. Also, impacting favourably on listing was the liberalisation of the Money Market in 1986 and the competitiveness of the Capital Market, induced issuance and listing activities, as many companies turned to the Capital Market for funds. Finally, increased public awareness about the market and privatisation by some state governments also contributed to the observed improvement in listing activities.

Equity Market Capitalisation in local currency terms has witnessed tremendous growth over the last six years, rising from ₦12.0 billion in 1990 to ₦61 billion in 1994 (408 per cent) and further to ₦223 billion by mid-August 1996 (266 per cent). Between December 1995 and mid-August 1996, Equity Market Capitalisation recorded an absolute increase of over ₦40.0 billion, or an average monthly rise of about ₦5.0 billion. In the last few years, equity market capitalisation has accounted for over 95 percent when interest bearing securities dominated the market.

The remarkable increase in market capitalisation in local currency terms is attributable to new listings which enhance market prices of equities. Unfortunately, the improvement in market capitalisation in local currency terms could not be matched in dollar terms as a consequence of the depreciation of the naira exchange rate. Thus, equity market capitalisation which recorded a growth of over 1,000 per cent between 1990 and 1995 in naira terms, witnessed an increase of only 48.0 per cent in dollar terms during the same period. By mid-August 1996, the Stock Exchange had a market capitalisation of about US$3 billion. If recent improvement in the náira exchange rate is sustained, the dollar value of the market capitalisation would equally improve and would enhance the attractiveness of the domestic market.

Nigerian has remained an attractive market in price index change (return). In 1994, it was a star performer, ranking second in the world with a growth of 168.8 per cent in US dollar terms; and so far this year, it has remained one of the top performing emerging markets. In spite of improvements in trading activities and market float in the past few years, the Nigerian Stock Market is still largely illiquid owing to a number of factors, including the absence of an efficient delivery system, supply inadequacy and the consequent tendency to buy high quality securities for keeps. However, the regulatory authorities are making efforts to improve liquidity by ameliorating these identified causes of the market's relative inactivity.

Capital markets are often assessed by their capability to efficiently mobilise and channel funds for project development, such as factory expansion and infrastructural facilities. At the development stage, the Nigerian Capital Market has performed this function well, providing many companies with long-term funds to finance various important projects in the country.

In the last decade, securities amounting to over ₦24 billion were issued by corporate entities giving an annual average of ₦2.4 billion while some States and Local Governments also successfully accessed the Market for funds to finance vital projects such as water systems, markets and housing estates. The total value of issues (Corporate and Government) in the last ten years was close to ₦30 billion.

Investor's acceptance of most Public Issues in the last six years has been quite impressive as evidenced by a study conducted by the SEC on the level of subscription to Public Issues during the reviewed period. The study revealed that on the average, Public Issues were 137.2 per cent subscribed (i.e. an oversubscription rate of 37.2 percent) which is indicative of the capacity and interest in the market.

Foreign Investment Through the Nigerian Capital Market

By definition, foreign investment is the acquisition of physical assets and/or securities by companies and nationals of one country in another. It is, in other words, a crossborder acquisition of financial or physical assets. The physical assets so acquired are usually in the form of factories, buildings, machinery, etc, for use in the production process and is referred to as direct investment. Direct investment involves the direct participation of a foreign company/national in the control and management of a domestic company (subsidiary). Ownership may be total, in which case the foreign company/national completely owns the assets of the domestic company. Where acquisition is partial, ownership and management of the company are shared between domestic and foreign companies/nationals. The level of control exercised by the shareholders in a partnership is usually dependent on the proportion of its holdings.

The acquisition of shares by foreign nationals or companies in a domestic Stock Market is known as foreign portfolio investment. Unlike direct investment, this type of investment does not usually involve the exercise of control over the company in which securities are acquired. Foreign portfolio investors are most often only interested in returns, capital gains and risk diversification. Therefore, where a company is perceived to be poorly managed, the typical portfolio investor would most likely adjust his portfolio by divesting his holding rather than interfering in its management. Being risk conscious, the typical foreign portfolio investor is not likely to hold significant stake in the securities of a company. Usually, the holdings would not exceed five per cent of the equity capital of a company, which in most cases is not large enough for control.

In addition to several socio-economic benefits, foreign portfolio investment is vital for the following reasons:

(i)   providing domestic companies with added opportunities for development capital;

(ii)   enhancing the performance of local Market Operators as they acquire more experience through international exposure;

(iii)   boosting the visibility and prestige of a Securities Market.

(iv)   diversifying the investor base of companies;

(v)   improving the debt/equity ratio of domestic companies;

(vi)   fostering appropriate pricing of securities as the financial sector becomes more efficient and liquid; and

(vii)   improving the liquidity of the domestic stock market.

Recapitalisation of Banks Through the Capital Market

In its circular dated 27th January, 1997, to all licensed banks, the Central Bank of Nigeria (CBN) considered the following modalities acceptable for the purpose of meeting the new minimum paid-up capital:

(i)   fresh injection of funds through a Rights Issue, Private Placement or Public Issue;

(ii)   capitalisation of appropriate reserves; and

(iii)   conversion of long-term loans and debentures into equity. A survey of the Market indicated that most banks are giving greater consideration to option (ii) and / or a combination of (i) and (ii).

However, except section 573, sub sections 1 and 2 of the Companies and Allied Matters Decree are amended, a public quoted bank is prohibited from doing a right issue. In the light of the foregoing, many banks may wish to raise funds through the Capital Market by issuing new shares to the public through an offer for subscription. Individuals as well as institutional investors will be free to invest by acquiring shares in the banks. Existing shareholders of the banks will be free to acquire more shares to enable them maintain reasonable percentage holding, if they so desire. The quantum of shares each bank will put on the capital market depends on the present market price of its shares and the amount expected. It is pertinent to highlight both the merits and demerits of this option. On the merit side, the option will inject the desired fresh funds which are required to meet the additional paid-up capital. The option also provides permanent fund which requires no repayment as in the case of debentures or preference shares. The option is relatively cheaper to package when compared to other forms of financing such as debenture.

If a bank's stock already commands high price in the Secondary Market, the nominal value of 50k per share sells well at a premium. If a bank is already saddled with expensive deposits, it will be in position to replace some of the deposits to reduce the interest expense and simultaneously improve its profit. Finally, the option will provide opportunity for few investors to come into the company.

Some of the demerits include dilution of ownership, the administrative cost of maintaining the shareholders' register will increase in view of the enlarged number of shareholders, diminution in the bank's per share ratios in the short run, and doubt of such success rate in view of the fact that shares of many banks will crowd the market due to the 1998 deadline set by government.

The second option referred to above, that is, capitalisation of reserves does not involve the role of the capital market. The use of this option is predicated on the fact that a bank has sufficient and appropriate reserves to capitalise. The merits of this option include immediacy of meeting the new minimum paid-up capital which will in turn boost the bank's corporate image and enhance its market perception, inexpensive to package as it involves very little expenditure except for the opportunity costs of losing the reserves, no dilution of existing shareholding structure, and shareholders will be happy. The demerit is that in all cases, the option does not provide new fund for working capital.

Another option is a mix of offer for subscription and the capitalisation of reserves. Some of the merits and demerits of options (i) and (ii) may be associated with this option.

To give effect to any of the options referred to above, the following statutory procedures are required:

(i) An Extra-ordinary General Meeting (EGM) of shareholders must approve the increase in the authorised share capital to a level over the above required minimum paid-up capital of ₦500 million.

(ii) Pass the necessary resolution at the EGM.

(iii) Register the newly created share capital and pay the required stamp duty.

Success Factor

The ability of any of the already quoted banks to raise additional funds from the Nigerian Capital Market depends on how well its stock has been performing on the Stock Exchange. The stocks of most of these banks might not have been bullish when assessed retrospectively but there is a rising profile of performance that depicts high prospects. Many of the banks have in recent times recorded rapid increases in their market prices indicating high demand for their stocks. This may be due partly to the fact that the banks have excellent performance for the previous year and partly due to the investor's expectation that many of these banks are likely to declare bonus to meet either wholly or part of the gap in the stipulated minimum capital requirement of ₦500 million. As earlier referred to in this chapter only one bank has so far met the requirement (March 1997).

Another critical success factor to consider is the liquidity potential of the investing public. In a situation where savings have been eroded due to high spending on consumption when viewed against the depreciated value of the naira and thus high inflation, less is left for investment in shares. The situation will be further complicated for the banks if all of them come to the market around the same time.

Listing of Non-Quoted Banks on the Nigerian Stock Exchange

There is no doubt that some of the unquoted banks will seek quotation on the Stock Exchange to raise additional capital. This may be done through introduction or by offer for subscription to the public. It must be emphasised that it is really one thing to get quoted on the Stock Exchange and another to command investors' confidence and that of the capital market as a quoted company.

In the last six years, as much as seven companies have been delisted from the Daily Official List of the Nigerian Stock Exchange, for reasons having to do with poor performance and post listing violations. In view of the harsh economic environment, one cannot predict from the onset whether a bank will default on its promises to its investors or capital market regulatory authorities. However, from records, some of the quoted banks, by their rare show of conservatism, astute management, corporate responsibility and dynamism, have become part of the group of reputable quoted companies in the Nigerian Capital Market. A recent case is the Guaranty Trust Bank Plc, which was listed by introduction in 1996. It is now one of the leading stocks in the banking sector of the Nigeria Stock Exchange.

Rules Governing Listing on the Nigerian Stock Exchange and Post –Listing General Undertaking

Any bank seeking quotations must be introduced to The Stock Exchange by a Dealing Member (Stockbroker) who acts as an intermediary between the bank and the exchange. His duty includes ensuring that all aspects of the issue comply with the Listing Requirements of the Exchange and other statutory provisions in the Securities and Exchange Commission Decree 1988, the Nigerian Enterprises Promotion Decree 1977 and the Companies Act 1968.

Table 7.2 General Requirements

First-Tier Market (MAIN)	Second-Tier Market (SSM)
1. Company must be registered as Public Limited Liability Co. under the provisions of the Companies & Allied Matters Decree 1990.	1. Company must be registered as Public Limited Liability Co. under the provisions of the Companies & Allied Matters Decree 1990.
2. Must submit to The Exchange financial Statement/business record of past 5 years.	2. Must submit to The Exchange financial Statement/business record of past 3 years
3. Date of last audited accounts must not be more than 9 months.	3. Date of last audited accounts must not be more than 9 months.
4. Amount of money that can be raised is unlimited depending on the borrowing power of the Director/Company.	4. Amount of money that can be raised may not exceed N10 million
5. Annual quotation fees based on market capitalisation.	5. Annual quotation fees is a flat rate of ₦5,000.00.
6. At least 25% of share capital must be offered to the public	6. At least 10% of share capital must be offered to the public
7. Number of shareholders must not be less than 300.	7. Number of shareholders must not be less than 100.
8. After listing, company must submit quarterly, half-yearly and annual accounts.	8. After listing, company must submit quarterly, half-yearly and annual accounts.

9. Securities must be fully paid up at time of allotment.	9. Securities must be fully paid up at time of allotment.
10. Unalloted securities must be sold on NSE trading floors.	10. Unalloted securities must be sold on NSE trading floors.
11. Provision for issue of mergers, acquisitions, unit trusts and mutual funds	11. No such provisions yet

It is pertinent to state here that both first and second-tier securities are subjected to the same dealing pattern on all trading floors of The Stock Exchange and market prices of each company appears on the Daily Official List of The Exchange.

Post-Listing Requirements

General/Listing Undertaking

A letter of Compliance or General Undertaking is a pledge by the agents or top management of the company or government agency, to abide by the Listing Requirements of The Exchange. The letter is normally brought in, signed by a Director and Secretary of the company to officials of The Exchange who then brief the Company Secretary on the rights and responsibilities of a publicly quoted company.

Returns to The Exchange

In the case of equities, the dictates of the General Undertaking requires the company to make certain periodic returns such as:

Interim Accounts – quarterly and half-yearly for first-tier companies and for second-tier companies, only semi-annual.

Final Accounts – both first and second-tier companies are required to submit their board-approved final audited accounts to The Exchange at the end of each company's financial year.

These accounts are subject to the security and approval of The Exchange before they can be published. The submission of the accounts, which is made available to stockbrokers on the trading floors, enables them to react to the interim and final performances of quoted companies.

In the case of debentures/bonds, no returns are currently made to The Exchange. It is the functions of the trustees to the bond issue to check on compliance with the terms and conditions of the debenture/bond issue. At maturity, the trustees must advise The Exchange on redemption in order to effect De-Listing of the Securities from the Official List of the Nigerian Stock Exchange.

It must be pointed out that the Listings, De-Listing and Suspensions are at the discretion of The Exchange.

Mergers

The prescribed capital requirement can be met by the merger of two or more banks. However it is advisable that banks planning to merge should ensure that there is complementarity in service and staffing to ensure survival and success after the merger. Mergers involving quoted banks must be cleared with both the SEC and NSE.

Emerging Funds

Investment Banking and Trust Company Ltd., recently floated a fund with an initial base of ₦1.5 billion. The fund is to be invested in the capital market, therefore institutions with good management and ready to conform with the discipline of the capital market could attract funds from such a source.

Sourcing for Funds From External Sources

Even though private investment continues to be financed largely by domestic savings, access to external sources of capital is playing a vital role in the private sector of developing countries. After the isolation experienced during debt crisis, the private sector in many developing countries now have access not only to renewed international debt markets, but also international equity markets; as source of new investment capital. Of notable relevance to Nigeria are portfolio investment and foreign direct investment.

Realising the fact that the absorptive capacity of the Nigerian Capital

Market cannot accommodate the total capital requirement of all the banks to be recapitalised, the need to look beyond the shores of this country has become imperative. Reference to Table 7.1 indicates that only five banks out of the thirty banks have foreign participation. This can be attributed to the adverse effects of the two past Indigenisation Decrees of 1977, and the restricted foreign exchange policy. Fortunately, bold steps have now been taken by government to create enabling environment for foreign investment to thrive. The Nigerian economy is today free of controls, market-led and consistent in policy, with greater recognition of the private sector as the engine of growth. The promulgation of two investment decrees viz, Investment Promotion Decree 16 of 1995 should be seen as providing opportunities or incentives to look beyond the domestic shores for the sourcing of fresh foreign capital, albeit by way of equity holding or debenture to finance corporate entities including banks in Nigeria.

The Sources of Capital from the International Capital Market

These include:

(a) Buy-Over or Acquisition

(b) Direct Investment

(c) Strategic Alliance

(d) Cross Border Bank Mergers and Acquisition

Buy-Over or Acquisition

In this arrangement, foreign investor(s) may acquire substantial or controlling interest in a bank thereby providing the required fund and concomitant direction for the bank.

A bank in Nigeria may explore merger or acquisition with another bank in the West African sub-region. Such crossborder merger or acquisition could boost the capital base of the Nigerian bank involved.

Direct Investment

In the case of direct investment as envisaged here, local investors will augment the capital of the bank with fund from foreign investors. The foreign investors may not be in controlling position, and may therefore just rely on the competence of local managers. The recent example is investment in the equities of United Bank for Africa Nigeria Plc through Global Depository Receipt (GDR). This is made possible as a result of globalization and liberalization.

Strategic Alliance

Strategic alliance can be in various forms between banks and/or non-bank financial institutions. The essential requirement for this type of arrangement is that it has to be mutually beneficial to parties involved.

International Finance Corporation

Over the years, the International Finance Corporation has invested and made available through financial intermediaries over $3.5 billion in the Finance and Capital Markets sector, covering more than 560 separate transactions to clients in over 50 countries.

The IFC Capital Market work includes – direct investments, underwriting and private placements, it has also pioneered a variety of investment funds in emerging markets. Among the funds promoted include country, regional and global funds, investing in listed securities in emerging markets, private equity and venture capital fund.

One of the most recent funds launched by IFC is the African Emerging Markets Funds (AEMF), the first investment fund targeted at securities listed on African Stock Markets. According to IFC report, the aim was to provide institutional investors with 'window' to invest in well managed private African firms. The same report stated that as at April 1996, the fund had invested in 86 stocks in fifteen African countries. Unfortunately, Nigeria was not among the countries where such investments were made. It is indeed true that opinion of foreign investors on Nigeria is not the best at this time (1997) but a bank that is properly structured and well packaged could access the fund.

Establishment of Closed or Open-Ended Funds Targeted at the Nigerian Market

A number of banks in alliance with some reputable fund managers abroad can explore the possibility of floating closed or open-ended fund targeted at the Nigerian Capital Market. Such a fund, if successfully launched can provide a large pool of fund for possible investment in the banking sector.

Fund Managers as Portfolio Managers in the International Capital Market

In accessing fund in the International Capital Market, it is essential to differentiate two category of managers. These are fund managers and portfolio managers. The distinguishing characteristics of the two are:-

Fund Managers: Fund managers like venture capitalists usually seek some control over investee firms. Such control include; taking board seats, providing advice and seeking to influence the managers of investee firms.

Portfolio Managers: These on the other hand seek no direct control over investee firms, they typically limit their exposure to any single firm.

Summary and Conclusion

The distress in the banking industry in the last five years ostensibly influenced the directive contained in the 1997 federal government budget that the minimum capital of both commercial and merchant banks should be increased to a uniform level of ₦500 million. The follow-up circular from the CBN to all licensed banks approved some options for the purpose of meeting the new minimum paid-up capital. These options include; fresh injection of capital through a rights issue, private placement or public issue, capitalisation of appropriate reserves, and conversion of long-term loans.

The role of the capital market, both domestic and international, becomes very crucial in the implementation of the first option. At the risk of stating the obvious, this chapter has explained in great details what the capital market is all about; also, how banks can explore both domestic and foreign sources of investment has been explained. The merits and demerits of sourcing funds through the capital market were also highlighted. One cannot conclude this chapter without mentioning factors which have important bearing upon a company's decisions to issue common stocks in order to raise capital. The important factors are:

(i)   risk sharing;

(ii)   dilution of ownership; and

(iii)   asymmetry of information.

In the light of the huge paid-up requirement of ₦500 million, the owners of many of the private banks will have a reservation price for bearing additional risk because they cannot achieve efficient risk diversification. The high reservation price for risk means that the banks will be less inclined to undertake investments with uncertain pay offs. This problem can be resolved by issuing new shares to the general public. This is where the capital market comes in. A wide ownership of the banks' common stocks allow for the associated risk to be spread across many stockholders.

An important disadvantage of issuing new shares, however, is the dilution of ownership. The ownership issue is probably the most important deterrent to going public or issuing additional shares. Balance has to be struck between risk diversification and ownership dilution. Guaranty Trust Bank set a very good example in 1996 in this direction.

Another factor involved is the regulatory and institutional issues. Going public requires full disclosure of information.

In conclusion, the role of the capital market is to mobilise resources and allocate them to the corporate sector in an efficient manner.

Chapter Six

Dealing in Securities and Maximising Investment Profit Through Trading in Rights Issues*

Benefits of Investing in Shares

Anyone can own a share. You may already be a share-owner without realising it as most life assurance companies and pension fund managers invest their customers' money on the Stock Market. Investment or dealing in shares can be risky, particularly in the short term. If the company you buy shares in, does badly, you could lose most or all of your money. But the potential gains are higher than the reward in other forms of investment. Over the years, two forms of long-term investment have done better than all others: house-owning and share-owning.

What Exactly is a Share?

A share is a part of a company, offered for sale to the public. The company is able to raise cash for expansion and new ventures by selling its shares to investors. Some companies – family businesses, for example – do not trade their shares. Firms that do are known as Public Limited Companies (Plc). Such companies seek listing on the Nigerian Stock Exchange, which is the market place for the shares of about 260 firms in Nigeria. Until recently, there was only one Stock Exchange in Nigeria,

---

Paper Presented at a Lecture Organised by Ibadan Zone, Shareholders' Association in March, 2001.

the Nigerian Stock Exchange. Abuja Stock Exchange has recently been established, and is now in full operation.

The first time it 'goes public' (also known as a **Flotation**), a company will often announce its intentions with advertisements in the press. This is called an **Offer for Sales or Initial Public Offering (IPO)**.

What Do You Get as a Shareholder?

As a shareholder, you are a part owner of the company and are entitled to take part in its decisions. You are sent an annual company report, you can vote on company issues; and you have the right to attend shareholders' meetings, like **Annual General Meeting** (AGM). If the company is doing well and makes profits, you benefit. Your shares should be worth more than when you bought them; and you may receive an income or **dividend** as well as participate in the rights issued by the company.

How Shareholding Can Make Money for You

A share's value is not fixed. Its price is determined by many things: the company's recent performance; the state of the sector of the economy the company trades in; national and international economic and political changes; the level of consumer demand; and the peculiarly unpredictable human factors of confidence and pessimism.

If you buy a share at one price and sell it at a higher price, you make a profit; if you sell it at a lower price, you make a loss. Shares can provide an income (though not necessarily a regular one) through the payment of dividend. However, a company can choose not to pay dividend at all, investing any profits back into the company. Dividend may be paid twice a year: the **Interim Dividend** and the **Final Dividend** as in the case of Nestle Nigeria Plc.

The company's share will sometimes show a rise in value just before the dividend dates, since the imminent income is attractive to buyers.

The price is usually brought back into line just after the dividend has been paid. There is an easy way of telling whether a share is available with or without a dividend payment; **cum div** means that the buyer will get the dividend, **ex div** means that the seller will have it. Also is **Ex. Sc.,** meaning After Scrip (Bonus) whereby it is the seller that will have bonus declared by the company.

How Stock Markets Work

In the same way that organised produce markets were set up for buying and selling commodities, so also were Stock Markets established for buying and selling securities, i.e. shares and bonds. The Stock Market is a perfect market that provides companies and governments with medium to long-term capital. The market consists of the suppliers of medium to long-term capital on one hand and those requiring such capital on the other hand. The two sectors, commonly referred to as surplus and deficit sectors, are connected by a number of intermediary organisations usually of a specialist nature.

Type of Shares

As a private investor in the Stock Market, you will almost always be dealing with what are known as **Ordinary Shares,** which make you a part owner of the business. You may come across other types such as **Preference Shares** which income is fixed. Their owners are entitled to receive dividends before the holders of ordinary shares. If a company is wound up, preference shareholders are paid first, after the creditors have been paid in full.

Buying Shares

Finding a Stockbroker

The current Nigerian Stock Exchange (NSE) Fact Book contains the list of approved registered Stockbroking firms in Nigeria. You may enlist the services of any of them. Some Stockbrokers will simply buy and sell shares at your request. This is called **Dealing Only** or **Execution Only**. The Capital Market regulatory authorities in Nigeria allow a graduated commission subject to a maximum of 2.75% of consideration. For an extra cost, you can ask a stockbroker for advice on what to buy and sell – that is, an **Advisory Service**. Or if you prefer to let your stockbroker buy and sell your shares – or **Portfolio** – without having to discuss every deal, you may choose a **Discretionary Service**, where your stockbroker simply sends you a regular statement, showing what has been bought and sold.

Choosing Your Share

When you give a stockbroker an order to buy or sell shares, that order is binding. Hence, if you use a dealing-only service, you must be absolutely sure of what you want. For steady long-term investment, you should consider **Blue Chip** shares. These are the shares of secure and respected Nigerian companies, many of which are household names: for example, Cadbury, Lever Brothers, P.Z., Nestle, Mobil, First Bank, Union Bank, Julius Berger etc. The term 'blue chip' derives from the highest value chip in a game of poker. You are unlikely to see spectacular increases in their share prices, but it is likely that over a number of years they will earn steady profits for shareholders.

Whatever type of shares you are looking for, you should cultivate the habit of reading the financial pages of daily newspapers. It is also helpful to talk to friends or colleagues about how they chose the shares they own. Remember, though, that the past record of a company cannot be taken as a guarantee of its future success.

The Price of Shares

Two prices are always quoted: the **Offer Price** (the higher price, and the one at which you buy shares), and the **Bid Price** (the lower price, and the one at which you sell shares). The price you will usually see quoted, in the newspapers for example, is the closing price for transactions on the previous day.

What to Look for in the Daily Official List of the Nigerian Stock Exchange (NSE)

Here is an example of what you might see if you turned to the Daily Official List of the NSE or the financial page of any Nigerian newspaper for share price information. The column headings in most newspapers will look pretty similar to this, although the company is fictional.

Ordinary Share	Public Quotation Price (₦)	Current Market (₦)	This High	Year's Low	Last Ex-Sc	Dividend Final	E.P.S	P.E Ratio
Unity Insurance Plc	0.50	2.91	3.67	2.91	16/10/00	0.30	0.30	22.3

The first column is the name of the stock, the second column indicates the normal or book value per share, the third column shows the previous day's market price, the fourth column shows the highest price in Naira that Unity Insurance attained in the year, the fifth column reflects its lowest price in the year. The sixth column shows when last the company declared bonus, the seventh column shows last dividend paid by the company, the eight column refers to the earnings per share which is the total earnings of the company divided by its number of shares. In the final column is the Price Earnings Ratio. A company's earnings are its income after tax in a financial year.

$$\text{P/E ratio} = \frac{\text{Current market price of company's share}}{\text{Company's earnings per individual share}}$$

Generally, the higher the P/E ratio, the more investors confidence in a company; but such confidence may not necessarily be justified. Sometimes, low P/E ratios are taken to mean that a company is undervalued; again, this may not be the case – the company could simply be poorly run and going nowhere.

It is important to compare P/E ratios within sectors to get an accurate idea of how the company is viewed. Do not for instance, compare a manufacturing company to one in banking.

Instructing Your Stockbroker

If you decide that you want to do it alone with a Dealing-Only Service, and you have worked out what shares you want to buy, you can tell your broker to buy **at Best** (also called **Best Price**), or you can set a **Limit Order**. 'At best' is the most common way to buy. It means the cheapest price that can be found for the share at the time you place your order, though that could be more than you were expecting to pay.

A limit order sets a maximum share price at which you are willing to let your broker buy. Usually, limit orders are only valid for a set period – for example, 30 days – and are restricted to deals over a certain size.

Becoming the Owner of the Shares

You are the owner of the shares as soon as the deal is reflected in your favour on the Central Securities Clearing System (CSCS). The CSCS will instruct the company's registrar to add your name to its share register. Your stockbroker will forward to you the **Contract Note.** This will show the number of shares you have bought, the price at which they were bought and all fees charged.

Your Privileges as a Shareholder

As a shareholder you will be first in line when a **Rights Issue** is announced. This happens when a company issues a new set of shares, in order to raise money. You will normally be offered a good deal on these new shares if you want to increase your existing shareholding in the company. The shares will be offered below the market price. As with the dividend, a company's shares will be quoted **cum rights** or **ex rights,** depending on whether the buyer or the seller will benefit from a rights issue.

You may also come across a **Capitalisation Issue** (also called a

Bonus Issue or a **Scrip Issue**). This is the case where a company gives extra shares to existing shareholders. A 1-for-1 scrip would give you two new shares for one old share; a 10-for-1 scrip would give 11 new shares for one old share. Owning more shares doesn't always make you richer, because as the number of shares increases, the value of each falls. One share might cost ₦6 before a 1-for-1 scrip issue, and ₦3 after; but you would have two for every one you had before. However, you may see an increase in the share price. Shares are described as **cum cap** or **ex cap** depending on whether the buyer or seller will benefit from a capitalisation issue.

Selling Shares

You do not have to use the same stockbroker as before, but you still need to go through a stockbroker. You need to be able to produce your share certificate or CSCS statement in the system for shares and sign a **Transfer Form,** both of which you return to your stockbroker. Your stockbroker sells the shares at best price or with a limit order (meaning that if he or she fails to obtain a minimum amount set by you, no sale will be made). Within a few days you will receive a contract note detailing the number of shares sold, the price at which they were sold and all fees charged.

Trading in Rights

Rights Issue, involved the provisional allotment of shares of a company to its existing shareholders in proportion of their holdings. This is one of the ways by which a company can increase its share capital, and it is only fair that existing members should be given the opportunity of increasing their holdings. Apart from increased holdings however, there are other benefits that may be enjoyed by shareholders under the new guidelines for trading in rights.

Stockbrokers play a significant role in assisting shareholders in profiting from their investments. Without the advice of stockbrokers, shareholders may miss a lot of their benefits especially on Rights Issues. It may be pertinent at this juncture to enumerate briefly the role of stockbrokers on the new procedure for trading in Rights and identify the advantages vis-à-vis the old system. It must however be appreciated that only the Rights Issues by quoted companies can be traded on the floor of the Exchange.

The Rights Issuing Company

Any company making Rights Issue will appoint a stockbroker for professional advice and marketing. The appointed stockbroker being a party to the Issue will obtain the Stock Exchange approval for the Issue and ensures that the Rights Circular and newspaper advertisement clearly state that the Rights could be traded between the opening and closing dates.

How to Sell Rights Shares

On receipt of Rights Circular and acceptance forms, a rational investor should consult his stockbroker for advice on whether to accept or sell/renounce his Rights. If he chooses to sell all or part of his Rights, he would be advised to take the following steps.

(i)   Complete the acceptance/renunciation columns of the form indicating the amount of Rights accepted and/or renounced.

(ii) Obtain a transfer form from his stockbroker for completion.

(iii) Complete the transfer form for the number of shares to be sold. (The number of shares to be sold is the same as the number of rights renounced).

The stockbroker will in turn forward the completed transfer form and the provisional allotment form to the Company Registrar for verification. If found okay, the stockbroker will proceed to sell on the floor of the Exchange.

Proceeds of Sale

Rights Issue price is usually lower than the current market price. To encourage shareholders who may wish to sell their rights, therefore, a bid/offer price would be fixed between the rights issues price and the market price. Since the provisionally allotted rights share were not paid for by the selling shareholder, it is only the difference between the rights price and the bid/offer price that the stockbroker would pay him. Proceeds of the rights price would be remitted to the issuing company.

An example is the provisional allotment of 10,000 rights shares of XYZ Plc allotted to Mr. D. at a rights Issue price of ₦3.00. The market price is ₦3.50 while the bid/offer price stands at ₦3.40. If Mr. D. sells his rights, he will receive only ₦4,000, that is, (₦3.40 – ₦3.00) x ₦10,000) from the stockbroker while ₦30,000 (₦3.00 x ₦10,000) will go to company (XYZ).

Buyer of Rights

If someone is not a shareholder of a company that is issuing Rights, and he is interested in the company's shares, he should contact a stockbroker who would bid for the shares on his behalf. All he needs to do is to complete a transfer form and pay the Rights Issue price plus the Bid price difference to the stockbroker. Using the example of Rights Issue of XYZ Plc mentioned above, the buyer now referred to as Mrs. K. will pay (₦34,000, that is, ₦3.00 x ₦10,000) + 40k x ₦10,000 to the stockbroker for disbursement).

Rights Trading Period

Whenever a company issues Rights that could be traded, the Exchange normally creates a special market for the daily trading between 10.00a.m and 10.30a.m. until the closure date. During this period, the stockbroker will market the shares between the company's existing shareholders and non-shareholders. Because of the limited time, prospective sellers and buyers of rights are advised to contact their stockbrokers before the closure date.

Subscription Returns

Rights acceptance forms (fully/partial) collected by stockbrokers are compiled and forwarded to the issuing houses or registrars together with subscription money after the closure date.

Listing of Rights Shares

At the end of the exercise, and after compliance with all requirements, the stockbroker to the issue will arrange for the listing of additional shares issued on the Stock Exchange. The company's share capital will thus be updated.

Old System versus the New Procedure

Prior to the formation of the present system of trading in Rights, once a shareholder cannot afford the payment for his Rights, he has no option other than to throw the provisional allotment form away. Today, that form can be converted to money.

Non-shareholders in a company that is issuing Rights cannot benefit from the reduced price under the old system. This situation has now changed for the better.

Going by our example of XYZ Plc, under the old system, the following scenario would arise in respect of this single shareholder.

(i)   The shareholder not taking his rights would lose ₦4,000.00.

(ii)   The buyer would lose ₦1,000.00 since he would have been forced to buy at the market price instead of Rights Bid price.

(iii)   The issuing company would suffer under subscription which may have to be taken care of by the Issuing House through warehousing or the existing shareholder taking additional shares freely.

(iv)   Returning centres would have lost the brokerage commission of ₦100 being 1% of ₦10,000.00.

Chapter Seven

Assisting Public Sector Resource Managers to Access Capital Market: The Role of a Stockbroker*

Introduction

Traditionally, State and Local Governments derive their revenue from two main sources:

   (1)   Statutory allocations from the Federal Account; and

   (2)   Internally–generated revenue from personal income tax, tenement rate, licensing fees, fees from commercialised public facilities (motor parks, markets, abattoirs etc) and investment income.

These resources are invariably inadequate in meeting the needs of the desired industrial and socio-economic infrastructural development. It is also noteworthy that even though, in nominal terms, the State/Local Governments are getting more from the Federation Account, when viewed against the depreciated value of the naira (₦), the purchasing power of such funds has in fact declined. To compound the situation, credit from the banking system is virtually drying-up due to the public sector's poor track record of debt servicing and repayment, a situation which has contributed significantly to the distress syndrome in the financial sector. To date, well over ₦9 billion is owed to banks by State Governments, repayment of which is feasible only if the banks are

Paper Presented at a National Conference on Private Sector Investment in Ekiti State, Organised by Total Communications Ventures, December, 2000.

prepared to grant substantial interest waiver. Interestingly, most of the banks in this predicament are State-owned. Given this experience, there is need for greater discipline and respect for commercial contractual terms in financial transactions entered into, by State and Local Governments.

In order to remedy this funding gap, State and Local Governments have to seek alternative sources of fund for the financing of key and viable projects. These projects should, of course, provide substantial socio-economic benefits to a wide spectrum of the populace. The logical areas include potable water, development of markets, motor parks, housing, garbage disposal, etc. As much as possible, it should be possible to cover the investments, through the introduction of user charges e.g. tolls collected on some highways, and very recently charges for water as is the case in Lagos State.

The Nigerian Capital Market, though still in the development stage offers viable financing opportunities for these socio-economic infrastructure. At this point, it would be appropriate to provide a brief review of the market.

The Nigerian Capital Market

Like any other capital market elsewhere in the world, the Nigerian Capital Market exists to provide long-term capital for economic and infrastructural development. The capital market instruments include equities (ordinary shares) and bonds. It can be differentiated from the money market in terms of the maturity profile of the instruments issued and traded. The money market essentially consists of such short-tenured instruments, often of less than one-year maturity such as Bankers Acceptance, Commercial Papers and Treasury Bills.

The capital market can be subdivided into two: the primary market which deals with initial public offerings and rights, and secondary market where securities are continuously traded between current holders (sellers) and buyers. Proceeds of such secondary trading transactions do not go to the primary issuer. The two levels of the market complement each other. While, the primary market feeds the secondary market with new securities, the success of these securities depends to a large extent on the receptivity in the secondary market and the liquidity it provides. Because of the flexibility of the capital market in terms of type and tenure of instruments, it ensures that the investment preferences of both lenders and borrowers are satisfied.

The capital market is not a single entity. Its structure consists of a network of specialised financial institutions that bring together suppliers and users of capital. These institutions include:

(1)   Companies and public sector borrowers

(2)   Issuing houses

(3)   Stockbroking firms

(4)   Merchant banks

(5)   Registrars

(6)   Individual and institutional investors (pension funds and insurance companies,

(7)   Unit Trusts

(8)   The Central Bank

(9)   The Securities and Exchange Commission

(10) The Stock Exchange

(11) Other professionals (Auditors, Solicitors, Valuers, etc.)

To ensure that transactions are conducted in an orderly, transparent and efficient manner and that investors are duly protected from unwholesome acts, the market has an elaborate legal framework consisting of relevant laws and regulatory institutions.

Specific governing laws include:

(i)   Companies and Allied Matters Decrees, 1990

(ii)   The Securities and Exchange Commission Decree, 1979 (re-enacted 1988)

(iii)   The Lagos Stock Exchange Act, 1961

(iv)   Trustee Investments Act, 1962

(v)   Income Tax Management Act, 1961

(vi)   Government and other securities (Local Trustees Powers) Act, 1957.

Regulatory Authorities in the Nigerian Capital Market

The two major regulatory bodies for the Capital Market are:

(1) *The Securities and Exchange Commission (SEC):*

The Securities and Exchange Commission by law, is the apex regulatory organ of the capital market with wide powers vested in it to, among others, register and regulate Stock Exchanges, other capital market operators and new issues of securities.

(2) *The Nigerian Stock Exchange (NSE):*

The Nigerian Stock Exchange is the hub of the market. It provides the framework and facilities for trading of securities in the secondary market and also through its listing requirements, offer opportunities for companies and governments to list shares/bonds through new issues of securities in the primary market.

By way of historical perspective, the development of a formal capital market in Nigeria dates back to the establishment of the Lagos Stock Exchange in 1961 through the enactment of The Lagos Stock Exchange Act of 1961. The Exchange was promoted and pioneered through the efforts of the Central Bank and the organised private sector. In 1977, based on the report of the Okigbo Committee on Financial System Review, The Lagos Stock Exchange was renamed Nigerian Stock

Exchange and subsequently embarked on the opening of branches/ trading floors in Kaduna (1978), Port Harcourt (1980), Kano (1989), Onitsha (1990), Ibadan (1990). Abuja branch was in the pipeline. It should be noted however that while a formal structure was established in 1961 for the trading in shares, Nigerians before this date, bought shares in companies promoted by both foreigners and Nigerians. In fact, as far back as 1946, public debt was funded through the issue of a 300,000 pounds (₦600,000) local loan stock bearing a coupon of 3 1/4 % and a maturity of 10-15 years. The issue was oversubscribed but largely by foreign investors. Other landmark events in the growth and development of the Nigerian Capital Market over the last 35 years include:

(i)   The Income Tax Management Act 1961, The National Provident Fund Act 1961, Trustee Investment Act 1962 and Insurance Act 1976. A Decree, in 1991 set out that 55% of insurance revenue should be invested in quoted corporate securities.

(ii)   The Nigerian Enterprises Promotion Decree of 1972 and 1977: these ensured wide participation in share ownership by Nigerians by dramatically boosting the supply of quoted securities.

(iii)   The transformation of the Capital Issues Committee into a full fledged Securities and Exchange Commission in 1979.

(iv)   The introduction of the Second-tier Securities Market (SSM) in 1985 to cater for small/medium scale indigenous enterprises seeking investment capital beyond the capacity of the original individual promoters.

(v)   The privatisation programme of 1989, which was responsible for the listing of 31 new companies on The Exchange.

(vi)   The Nigerian Investment Promotion Decree No. 16 of 1995 and the Foreign Exchange (Monitoring and Miscellaneous Provisions) Decree No. 17 of 1995, which replaced the repealed Nigerian Enterprises Promotion Decree and the Exchange Control Act 1962.

(vii)   Investment and Securities Decree, 1999.

Using the Capital Market to Finance State and Local Government Projects

The need to supplement their internally-generated sources of revenues has become imperative for State and Local Governments to look outwards for additional sources of funding to close their resource gaps. Under this circumstance, the capital market appears a good option since the banking industry is not the ideal source for long term funds.

The advantage that will accrue to State and Local Governments which patronise the capital market are many. One, more capital projects will be executed as more resources are available for government capital expenditures. Two, there will be better accountability for use of funds as statutory financial reports must be produced regularly on projects funded by the market. Three, raising funds from the capital market will release government subvention for special projects.

Finally, the tendency to spend money on "white elephant projects" will be curtailed as only economically viable projects could be financed from the capital market.

Projects may be promoted through:

(a) Government undertaking it directly;

(b) State corporation or parastatals;

(c) The formation of a limited liability company by government which will handle the project on its behalf;

(d) A joint venture between government and other investors; and

(e) Build, Operate and Own (BOO) or Build, Operate and Transfer (BOT).

Principal Features of Government Borrowings

Borrowings by the state, local and other government agencies are governed by the provisions in part (xii) of the Investment and securities Act No. 45 of 1999. Some of the principal features are:

(i)   that the total amount of loans outstanding at any particular time including the proposed loan shall not exceed fifty percent of the actual revenue of the issuing body for the preceding years.

(ii)   the issuer should support its application with an original copy of an irrevocable letter of authority giving the Accountant General of the Federation the authority to deduct at source from the statutory allocation due to the issuer, in the event of default in meeting its payment obligation under the terms of the loan and the trust deed.

(iii)   A copy of the Irrevocable Letter of Authority shall be lodged with the trustees appointed under the relevant provisions of the Act.

(iv)   The principal repayment source for the principal and interest payment shall be from the general revenue and assets of the issuer concerned and of the assets of the appropriate authority or project which is the beneficiary of the proceeds of the loan.

(v)   Any public issue of securities or bond by a public sector body shall have a maturity not exceeding twenty-five years from the date of issuance of the registered bond or securities.

(vi)   All issues by a public sector body shall be in registered form and the interest due on such registered bonds shall be payable half yearly or quarterly on the dates specified in a trust deed.

(vii)   A **Registrar** must be appointed to keep a register for recording all securities transaction including the names and addresses of the bond holders and the persons deriving title therefrom, the amount of securities held by every holder, and the date the name is recorded in the register. Every bond holder is entitled to receive from the Registrar, a bond certificate indicating the amount of his/her holding.

(viii)   A **Trustee** must be appointed and shall have all the powers conferred upon Trustees by the Trustees Investment Act.

(ix)   A separate **sinking fund** shall be created for each loan raised. A biannual or quarterly contribution shall be made to the sinking fund for the purpose of redeeming the loan. All such contributions to the sinking fund established for any loan shall be paid to the Trustees whose responsibility is to manage the fund. All such moneys realised by way of dividends, interest, bonus and other profit of any investment shall be invested by the trustee to form a part of the sinking fund.

(x)   In case where the issuer is unable to meet its payment obligation under the loan and after the expiration of six months therefrom, the Trustees shall present the copy of the Irrevocable Letter of Authority to the Accountant General of the Federation who shall take immediate steps to deduct the appropriate amount from the statutory allocation of the issuer.

Raising Funds from the Capital Market

Funds can be raised by public issue or private placement. Public Issue is for the general public, although it is not unusual to provide preferential allotment of shares or bonds to some specific people. This will encourage an organised secondary market for the sale of the securities.

Specifically, options available to State and Local Governments to raise funds in the capital market include, amongst others:

(i) Bond financing

(ii)   Securitisation

(iii)   Privatisation

(iv)   Build, Operate and Own

(v)   Build, Operate and Transfer

Bonds as a Financing Option

Public bodies can raise two types of bonds:

(a) General obligation bonds and

(b) Revenue bonds

The first is for the financing of the general obligation (working capital) of the government and is secured by the full faith and credit of the government. The primary source of repayment is from the general revenues – taxes, levies, dues, rates – of government.

The revenue bonds are tied to the revenues from the projects for which they were raised; in a way, these are self-financing or liquidating. Though various state governments have issued revenue bonds in the market, these are not strictly revenue bonds as many of the projects could hardly qualify in terms of generating adequate revenues for the repayment. So, in most cases, the repayment is from the general revenues of the State or Local Governments.

The Federal and State Governments are no strangers to the capital market. Right from the inception of the market, many Federal Government development projects have been financed by the capital market through the issue of Federal Government Development Stocks. Currently, there are about 28 Federal Government Development Stocks quoted on The Exchange, with five State Government bonds and one Local Government bond, namely:

1.   Ogun State Government (₦30 million revenue bonds in 1987 for Abeokuta Water Scheme).

2.   Lagos State Government (₦30 million revenue bonds in 1987 for Lekki Peninsula).

3.   Bendel State Government (₦50 million revenue bonds in 1978).

4.   Kaduna State Government (₦50 million for ginger processing plant).

5.   Lagos State Government (₦90 million in 1990, Lekki Peninsula).

6.   Edo State Government is the latest in accessing capital market.

In 1992, Lagos Island Local Government became the first Local Government to approach the Capital Market for a ₦100 million revenue bond to finance the construction of a shopping centre.

In all these cases, and as a general rule, the State/Local Government enjoys such advantages as:

(1)   Freeing-up subvention funds for other pressing needs e.g. education and health-care delivery services.

(2)   Providing more services to the populace as more projects can be embarked upon.

(3)   Inculcating financial discipline/accountability on public sector managers as the borrowed funds are tied to specific projects and repayment is monitored by Trustees and regulatory agencies. The urge to embark on "white elephant" projects is thus reduced.

(4)   Savings through cheaper costs associated with bond issue as against bank borrowing.

Before we examine the underlying modalities of a bond issue by a State/Local Government, let us briefly review the nature of the instrument itself.

A bond is defined as a long-term interest bearing promissory note or IOU, wherein the issuer (borrower) undertakes to pay the interest portion periodically and the principal at some specified future date (final maturity).

A bond may be secured or unsecured and borrowers/issuers

frequently issue both types. Where the bond is secured, it is charged on certain specific assets of the borrower which the bond holders can look forward to for repayment in the event of the issuer defaulting. This is usually referred to as a mortgage debenture or bond. On the other hand, unsecured bond holders rank equally with ordinary creditors of the issuer of the bond. Some major features of bonds are:

(1)   Long-dated (often exceed five years in tenure)

(2)   Involve very substantial amounts

(3)   Issued in large denominations

(4)   Interest paid quarterly, half yearly or yearly.

Given these features and the widespread holding of bonds, it is important to establish communication between bondholders and the borrower. A trust deed is often drawn-up between the borrower and a trustee, setting out clearly the terms of the issue, the security charged and the powers in respect of the bond.

Types of Government Bonds

Governments; Federal, State or local can raise finance through the issuance of a variety of bonds . Some possibilities are given below:

Revenue Bonds

(i)   *Airport Revenue Bonds based on the traffic-generated revenues that result from the competitiveness and passenger demand of the airport.*

Revenues from the airport may come from landing fees paid by the airlines for their flights, concession fees paid by restaurants, shops, newstands, and parking facilities, and from airline apron and fuelling fees.

Another form of airport revenue bond is one secured by a lease with one or more airlines for the use of a specific facility such as a terminal or hangar. The lease usually obligates them to make annual payments sufficient to pay the expenses and debt service for the facility.

(ii) Highway Revenue Bonds

There are two types. The first can be used to build specific revenue-yielding facilities such as toll roads, bridges, and funnels. The financial soundness of the bonds depends on the ability of the specific projects to be self-supporting. Proceeds from the second type of highway revenue bond generally are used for public highway improvements and the bondholders are paid by earmarked revenues such as gasoline taxes, automobile registration payments, and drivers' licence fees.

(iii) Hospital revenue Bonds

The security is usually dependent on the issuing government or subvention or reimbursement from higher level government, and individual patient payments.

(iv) Housing Revenue Bonds

There are two basic types of housing revenue bonds, each with a different type of security structure. One is the housing revenue bond secured by single-family mortgages, and the other is the housing revenue bond secured by mortgages on multifamily housing projects.

(v) Industrial revenue Bonds

They are generally issued by state or local governments on behalf of individual companies and businesses. The security for the bonds usually depends on the economic soundness of the particular company or business involved.

(vi) Public Power Revenue Bonds

These are issued to finance the construction of electrical generating plants. An issuer of the bond may construct and operate one power plant, buy electric power from a wholesaler and sell it retail, construct and operate several power plants or join with other public private utilities in jointly financing the construction of one or more plants. They are secured by revenues to be produced from the operating plants.

(vii) Lease - Rental Bonds

These are issued to finance public purposes such as public office buildings, fire houses, police stations, University buildings, mental health facilities, and highways, as well as office equipment and computers. In some instances, the payments may come from student tuition, patient fees, and earmarked tax revenues, and the state or local government is not legally obligated to make lease-rental payments beyond the amount of available earmarked revenues. However, the lessee state is usually required to make payment from its general fund subject to annual legislative appropriation.

(viii) Water and Sewer revenue Bonds

These are issued to provide for a local community's basic needs and as such are not usually subject to general economic changes. It is required that user charges cover operating, maintenance and approximately 1.2 times annual debt-service and reserve requirements.

(ix) College and University Revenue Bonds

The revenue-securing College and University revenue bonds usually include dormitory room or hostel rental fees, tuition payments, and sometimes the general assets of the College or University as well.

Sinking Fund Arrangement

This is a common feature of many corporate and government bonds. It is designed to ensure an orderly retirement of the debt by the issuer. Specific amounts are set aside in an account usually yearly and the funds managed by the trustee. The Sinking Fund and continuing redemption arrangement is considered an additional protection for investors and the bond is therefore perceived to be of a lower risk. The existence of the fund therefore enhances a bond's market rating and marketability.

While most of the bonds raised in the market were applied largely to fund socio-economic infrastructure, we must also be aware that they can be used to finance industrial projects as well. This can be achieved where government floats companies in partnership with the private sector. Bond issue proceeds can then be used to pay for government's equity contribution in such companies. It is however desirable, given the benefit of hindsight, that management of the companies be free of government interference. These joint venture companies can then develop on their own, and at a suitable time approach the market for listing to source additional funds for expansion. Governments can also use proceeds from bonds to finance the development of industrial estates where all relevant services are provided.

Modalities

To proceed on a bond-raising exercise for a State/Local Government, it is important that the following steps be taken:

(i)   Establish the limitations (if any) of the Government to raise loan capital in the manner envisaged. The consent of the Federal Ministry of Finance to the State/Local Government to borrow must be obtained.

(ii)   Enactment of the relevant enabling law (edict) authorising the borrowing. The edict will of course be gazetted and a copy of this will accompany the application to NSE and SEC.

(iii)   Guarantee of a third party (if necessary) for the repayment obligations.

(iv)   Approval (if required) from the supervising Government ministry.

(v)   Incorporation of a limited liability company if the borrowing is for a commercial project and the assets are to be used as security.

(vi) Establish source of repayment. For example, repayment may be tied to income from a specific State/Local Government account e.g., its share of the Federation Account.

(vii) Determine whether the project will be handled by the State Government directly, a State Government Parastatal/ Corporation, a limited liability company, or a joint venture between the Government and other investors.

(viii) Prepare a project Feasibility Study/Report which will indicate among others the financing structure. If a limited liability company/joint venture approach is to be adopted, equity funds will be required.

(ix) Appointment of an Issuing House.

Other parties required in addition to the Issuing House for the consummation of the exercise include:

(1) Stockbrokers to the Issue

(2) Auditors

(3) Reporting Accountants

(4) Solicitors to the State/Local Government

(5) Solicitors to the Trustees

(6) Solicitors to the Issue

(7) Trustees

(8) Registrars

(9) Portfolio Managers

The Issuing House

As in all public issue of securities, the Issuing House often doubles as the financial adviser and co-ordinator of the capital-raising exercise. It drafts the prospectus, negotiates terms of issue with the issuer, co-ordinates the activities of all other parties to the Issue, organises the all-parties meetings, liaises between the issuer and the regulatory bodies – The Nigerian Stock Exchange, through the Broker to the Issue and the Securities and Exchange Commission – and plays the leading role in the marketing of the Issue. The success of an Issue therefore rests to a large extent on the reputation of the Issuing House. A reputable Issuing House should possess strong documentation, placement and underwriting capacities.

Documentation and Listing Requirements for State/Local Government Bonds

In addition to the listing requirements for corporate bonds, State/Local Governments seeking to raise funds from the Capital Market through revenue bonds must provide the following:

(1)   Profile of the State or Local Government, providing demographic information (population, location, industries etc.)

(2)   Legal authority for the Issue (State legislation).

(3)   Feasibility study for the project to be financed as all bonds should be project-tied.

(4)   Federal Minister of Finance consent to the Issue

(5)   State/Local Government's five year audited accounts. If it is a beneficiary company, its five years audited accounts.

(6)   The prospectus, which must contain:

(i)   Full name of the issuing company or organisation;

(ii)   Amount and title of the Issue;

(iii)   Price of the Issue;

(iv)   Written undertaking that application has been made to the Exchange for quotation of the security;

(v)   Opening and closing dates of subscription including management/directors;

(vi)   Trustees' status;

(vii)   Parties to the Issue, etc.

(7)   Statement by the Accountant-General that to the best of his knowledge and belief, there is nothing contained or omitted in the prospectus which will make the statements misleading.

(8)   Memorandum/Articles of Association of beneficiary company.

(9)   Certificate of Incorporation of beneficiary company.

(10)   Relevant resolution passed by the board.

(11)   Draft Trust Deed.

(12)   Letter of authority from the State/Local Government to the Central Bank that in case of default, the bond principal and interest are to be deducted from their Statutory Allocation Account and paid over to the Trustees. The Central Bank of Nigeria must accept this in writing and to evidence same, will issue a Letter of Consent.

Securitisation

Another important area where the Capital Market can be of immense benefit to Government is the securitisation of domestic debts owed by State Governments to banks, contractors and suppliers. These public debts remain largely unserviced. The adverse effects of such debts on the economic health of this nation cannot be overstated. A situation where contractors utilise their working capital and/or borrow to execute state contracts and remain unpaid can create avoidable tension and compromises among individuals, as well as small and medium-sized companies. The same is true for banks that, as a result of non-payment, have to make huge provision for bad and doubtful debts under the Prudential Guidelines. Government should therefore look at options to liquidate certified domestic debts. One such option is the securitisation of these debts which has the added benefit of promoting a bond market.

Towards this end, the Securities and Exchange Commission and the Nigerian Stock Exchange in June 1996 organised a two-day seminar in Lagos titled: "Securitisation of Domestic Public Debts." The Central Bank of Nigeria also organised a similar seminar in October 1997.

Securitisation is a recent innovation on the international capital market scene. This financing technique was developed in the US where it has grown from a few million dollars worth of transaction in the 1970s into a trillion dollar market in recent times.

In simple terms, securitisation refers to raising on the finance strength of existing assets. An important asset of many financial institutions is the money they are owed by their customers. The eventual repayment of these loans represents a valuable store of future cashflow for which another borrower can often be found.

The process of securitisation is the repackaging of the accounting and legal form of receivables and loans into securities. It is the transformation of illiquid asset to a liquid asset. In other words, using securitisation, a worthy project will not be starved of funds simply because it is being promoted by the relatively unknown institution or because current regulation limits the amount of loan that can be advanced by banks. What matters is the quality of cashflows of the underlying assets.

The essential ingredients for the success of any securitisation exercise are not hard to fathom: the issues could be handled by the CBN, as is the case of Federal Development Stock issues; the pricing of the bonds should be realistic and attractive; and the bonds should have the same type of liquidity that other government debts have.

The Exchange in response to solving the problem of alleviating the burden of domestic sovereign debts in the books of banks, supports the securitization of such debts. Such arrangements will restore confidence in doing business with government, ease the burden of the liabilities of government to the banking industry, contractors and suppliers and liven the cashflow within the economy as investors holding such bonds will have a Stock Market to trade them on. This arrangement will provide a win-win game plan for the affected banks, governments, creditors and indeed the economy.

Privatisation

Privatisation is another option for reviving ailing public companies. In this regard, government can use its resources to complete the projects and thereafter recover such funds by offering the shares of the enterprise for sale in the Capital Market. Apart from releasing funds which can be recycled into new infrastructure and social projects, privatisation allows government to concentrate on the provision of public goods and services rather than actions that may be inflationary. Beyond this, recent privatisation experience in the country shows that the successful privatisation of any enterprise increases its operating efficiency and reduces its dependence on government subvention.

The Rolé of a Stockbroker

Having dwelt at length on the characteristics of the Capital Market and the opportunities which exist therein for investors and users of long-term funds, let me now briefly explain in general the specific role of a stockbroker. Stockbrokers are licensed by the Securities and Exchange Commission and the Nigerian Stock Exchange. They are dealing members of the Stock Exchange performing the following functions among others:

(a) Stockbrokers act as agents for the public, receiving and executing buy or sell orders for shares according to the instructions of their clients. For these services, they earn commission as laid down by the Exchange;

(b)   They perform advisory services to their clients in the selection and administration of their investments with a view to enabling their clients meet their investment objectives and also improve the performance of their portfolio.

(c)   Listing or quotation of company shares and stock on the Exchange are arranged by stockbrokers so that trading may commence on such security. The affected companies are charged a fee for this service.

(d)   Issuing House, if a stockbroker is so registered by SEC.

(e)   Special requests for share certificates or statements of holding from clients are processed through the CSCS to the Registrars.

(f)   Bids and offers are matched by stockbrokers on the trading floors of the Nigerian Stock Exchange every business day using Call-Over System between 11a.m. and 2p.m. The NSE is in the process of changing to ATS.

(g)   Pricing of new issues are determined by Issuing Houses/ stockbrokers while secondary Market prices are determined by stock.

Dealing with stockbrokers is strictly on **trust** as transactions are by verbal agreement which are later backed by documentation, hence their motto: "my word is my bond".

Conclusion

Statutory Allocation and internally generated revenue have proved inadequate for State and Local Governments; and bank borrowings, where feasible, are expensive as sources of financing their capital projects. State and Local Governments' officials need to acquaint themselves with utilisation and benefits of Capital Market instruments including municipal bond. Project-tied bonds floated on the Capital Market, apart from ensuring that the funding required is successfully raised, also subjects the recipient State and Local Governments to the transparency and financial discipline which the Stock Market imposes.

Finally, by relying more on the market, State and Local Governments will be less burdened by traditional sources of revenue for their capital projects, especially the commercially viable ones.

Chapter Eight

Effective Pricing of Securities in the Secondary Market*

Introduction

This chapter is a bold attempt to discuss an effective pricing of securities in the secondary market. Pricing of securities can be defined as the process of estimating the Return and Risk of a stock. When an investor parts with his resources for a stake in a particular company, he bears or carries some risks (of uncertainties) with him. As compensation, he expects a return on his investment. The risk is otherwise known as Variability of Returns.

The paradoxical assertion of Dr. Seuss (1979) on West Beast: East Beast is apt for our discussion in this chapter. He stated thus:

> Upon an Island hard to reach,
> The East Beast sits upon his beach.
> Upon the West beach sits the West Beast.
> Each beach Beast thinks he's the best Beast.

> Which Beast is best? ... Well, I thought at first
> That the East' was the best and the West' was worst.
> Then I looked again from the West to the East
> And I liked the Beast on the East beach least.

Paper Presented at the Technical Working Session for Students Preparing for CIS Examination held in Lagos on 9th May, 1999.

For everything that exists and finds its way to the market, there is a price attached to it. An interested institution can determine this price e.g. government, as is the case in the socialist economy or determined by the interaction of the forces of demand and supply as it is in the capitalist economy. These two ways of determining prices could be regarded as being on the extreme, thereby making possible a situation whereby a price is determined through the combined efforts of the two. In other words, we cannot shy away from the fact that there could be other contributory factors that impact on price determination apart from the forces of demand and supply or institution at interests.

Basically, in the capitalist economy, price determination/movement is subject to the working of the forces of demand and supply. When supply exceeds demand, price falls, otherwise, it rises.

Some of the time, price is considered by some as either too high while others deem it otherwise. A very good example of divergence in the pricing analysis is that of securities on the floor of the stock exchange where criticism often come from many quarters, some from senior executives of quoted companies, who at times feel their shares have been undervalued; both private and institutional investors; experts in securities pricing; stockbrokers (who sometimes think the price of a stock should move because their client demands for it for his own benefit or favour); and other interested observers of the Nigerian Capital Market.

An international observer from the World Bank once described the Call-Over system of the Nigerian Stock Exchange pricing technique as "literary and debating."

Theoretical Consideration

A widely accepted investment theory states that the value of a common stock is equivalent to the present value of a growing stream of future dividend payment and capital gains for a finite holding period. But for an infinite horizon, the value of a stock is simply the present value of an infinite stream of dividend only. This is because as the horizon recedes further into the future, the present value of the end-of-period price becomes very small and negligible. The value of the stock is made up only of the present value of the cumulative dividends. Therefore, to calculate the value of a stock on the basis of this theory, it is necessary to estimate the growth rate of the stock's dividend stream and to discount the estimated dividend at a rate deemed appropriate.

The present value theory can be applied with practical results to an appraisal of a general index of common stock prices (where such index exists as in the Nigeria Stock Exchange) or to estimating the value of individual common stocks, as revealed by Bing A. Ralph in his *Survey of Practitioners' Stock Evaluation Methods*, in 1971.

There exist two inherent difficulties associated with the theory:

(a) The determination of the growth rate of the stock's dividend stream, and

(b) The appropriate discount rate.

Some Present Value Determination

This involves the use of the discount table and the estimated future streams of dividend. Assuming that Ade wants to borrow money from Bello repayable at a future date, and Bello is willing to make the loan but feels that considering the risks involved, he is entitled to a 12 per cent annual rate of return. How much money will Bello advance to Ade on Ade's note for ₦100 payable in one year?

Using the present value table, the present value interest factor (PVIF) in one year at 12% discount rate is 0.8928. By multiplying ₦100 payable by the PVIF; . 8928* 100 = ₦89.28. Therefore, the present value of ₦100 due in one year is N89.28.

Let us assume further that the future dividends on the stocks in the NSE All Share Index will grow at a rate of 15% per annum, for as far into the future as anyone can imagine. Assuming also that investors, as a group, will demand at least 20% rate of return in order to undertake the risks of common stock investment, what would be the value of NSE All Share Index ? This can be determined through the use of a simple formula for approximating the present value of perpetual dividend growth at a given discount rate, thus:

$$\text{Present Value} = \frac{\text{Current Dividend Rate}}{\{(1 + \text{discount rate}) / (1 + \text{growth rate})\} - 1}$$

or

$$\text{Perpetuity Value of a given stream (V)} = \frac{D}{r - g}$$

Using the above illustration for this purpose, we have:

$$\frac{\text{Current Dividend Rate}}{\{(1.20/1.15) - 1\}} = \frac{\text{Current Dividend Rate}}{1.043 - 1} = \frac{\text{Current Dividend Rate}}{0.043}$$

From the above illustration with its underlying assumptions, it could be inferred that the appropriate current dividend yield of NSE index is 4.3%. Suppose the current dividend rate on NSE index was about 100, then

The present value would be $\dfrac{100}{0.43} = \underline{232.56}$

Since the actual level of the index for that year was just about 233, it can be concluded that under our illustrative growth and discount rate assumptions, the actual level of the market represented fair or intrinsic or normal value.

Let us consider how to arrive at realistic estimates of the growth rate of earnings and dividends and an appropriate discount rate.

Prospective Growth Rate

Studies in developed markets have shown some consistency in the rate of earnings growth and dividend growth, even though the rate may change slightly in some years. Within such a steady state, analysts have been able to make the conclusion that if earnings grow at a certain rate per annum, dividends should grow correspondingly. Thus, the growth rate is arrived at by multiplying earning retention ratio by return on equity (ROE).

Where:

$$\text{Retention Ratio} = 1 - \frac{DPS}{EPS}$$

$$ROE = \frac{NET\ INCOME}{TOTAL\ NO.\ OF\ SHARES\ ISSUED\ BY\ THE\ COMPANY}$$

$$\text{Payment Ratio} = \frac{DPS}{EPS}$$

As such, Growth Rate = ROE * RETENTION RATIO

If a security is expected to become more valuable in the future, this anticipated rise will tend to make it more valuable now. In order to place a current value on future growth in value, that growth must be estimated before it occurs.

The Choice of an Appropriate Discount Rate

There is need to have a clear idea of the rate of return investors require in order to undertake the risks of common stock investment.

In making this decision, two issues should be thoroughly borne in mind.

(a) The consideration is on the investors in the aggregate and not a single investor.

(b) The stocks are also considered in the aggregate as represented by a renowned investment Research House and not by any specific stock.

Three approaches have been found to be useful:

(i)   Annual rate of return on stockholders' equity.

(ii) Rate from the bond market, i.e. rate of return on risk-free fixed income investments, for example, long-term government bonds, and savings account institutions. To the rate chosen based on these rates, should be added a risk factor associated with common stock.

(iii) Historical average rate of return.

In undertaking this exercise, the analyst should be sure that his assumptions regarding real economic growth, inflation, corporate profit and dividend growth, interest rates and common stock discount rates are mutually consistent.

Approaches to the Evaluation of Individual Common Stocks

Since the concept of the present value of future dividends has proved useful in estimating the value of common stock prices in the aggregate, some attempts have been made at evaluating individual common stocks by some reasonable number of authors. Equally, some difficulties have been identified in evaluating individual common stocks.

(a)   It is more difficult to project the growth rate of an individual company than it is to project total corporate growth.

(b)   It is more difficult to select an appropriate discount rate for an individual company's estimated dividend stream than it is to select a rate for all corporations combined.

(c)   Since the discounting approach has been supported in terms of dividends rather than earnings, it is difficult to deal with the company that does not pay cash dividends.

The Use of Selling Price as a Proxy

Selling Price Projections

In lieu of the difficulties associated with making long-term dividend growth estimates, it is suggested that a selling price for some years in the future be assumed and discounted. For example, an analyst may project dividend growth for about ten years and assume some dividend yield at that date.

Earnings Projections

An alternative is to project earnings, assuming a constant dividend payout ratio and hypothesise an ultimate price-earning ratio. Some analysts project earnings and also allow for changes in dividend payout ratios.

It should be noted that the projected growth of a company whose past earnings have fluctuated substantially usually contain a greater element of uncertainty than the projected growth of a company with a record of stability.

Adjusting for Uncertainty via the Discount Rate

The more uncertain the growth projection, the higher the discount rate should be. Investors, generally, are believed to be "risk averters". The appropriate relationship between uncertainty and the discount rate is unclear. There are therefore inherent difficulties posed by the need to select different discount rates for different time periods in the growth cycle of any individual stock.

Forecasting Earnings and Price-Earning Ratio

Bonds

Bonds call for the payment of specified amount of interest for a stated number of years, and for the repayment of the par value on the bonds maturity date. A bond therefore represents an annuity plus a lump sum, and its value is found as the present value of this payment stream.

$$\text{Value} \quad = \quad \sum_{t=1}^{n} \frac{I_t}{(1+kd)^t} \quad + \quad \frac{M}{(1+kd)^n}$$

$$= \quad I_t(PVIFA_{kdn}) + M(PVIF_{kdn})$$

Where:

I_t = monetary value of interest paid each year = interest rate multiplied by par value

M = par value or maturity value, which is typically ₦1000

kd = appropriate rate of interest on the bond.

n = number of years until the bond matures, n declines each year after the bond is issued.

$PVIFA_{kdn}$ = Present Value Interest Factor of an Annuity, given cost of debt of the nth period.

$PVIF_{kdn}$ = Present Value Interest Factor, given cost of debt of the nth period.

Common Stock Valuation

Earlier on, we found the value of a bond as the present value of interest payments over the life of the bond plus the present value of the bond's maturity (or par) value. Stock prices are similarly determined as the present value of a stream of cash flows and the basic valuation equation is similar to the bond valuation equation.

Value of Stock = P_0 = Present value of expected future dividends

$$P_0 = \frac{D_1}{(1+k_s)} + \frac{D_2}{(1+k_s)^2} + \ldots + \frac{D_n}{(1+k_s)^n}$$

$$= \sum_{t=1}^{n} \frac{D_t}{(1+k_s)^t} \qquad \text{Here, n is infinite}$$

where k_s = expected rate of return

If n is finite, then

$$P_0 = \sum_{t=1}^{n} \frac{D_t}{(1+k_s)^t} + \frac{P_n}{(1+k_s)^n}$$

The value of a stock is the sum of the present value of the expected dividend streams plus the present value of the nth period price of the share.

Stock Value With Zero Growth (Perpetuity)

In this case, $D_1 = D_2 = D_3 = D_n$. So it is like an ordinary perpetuity and can be valued as a preferred stock.

$$P_0 = \frac{D}{(1+k_s)} + \frac{D}{(1+k_s)^2} + ... + \frac{D}{(1+k_s)^\infty}$$

$$P_0 = D/k_s$$

Normal, or Constant Growth

$$P_0 = \frac{D_0(1+g)}{(k_s-g)} = \frac{D_1}{(k_s-g)}$$

It is assumed that $g < k_s$, that is, the growth rate is less than the discount rate, otherwise P_0 will be infinite and no share sells at an infinite value.

Expected Rate of Return on the Constant Growth Stock

Expected Rate of = Expected Dividend + Expected Growth Rate
   Return   Yield   or Capital Gains Yield

$$K_s \quad = \quad D_1/P_0 \quad + \quad g$$

$$P_0 = \frac{D_1}{k_s-g}$$

The rate of growth in dividend will be identical to the rate of growth in share price.

Variable Growth

$$P_0 = \sum_{t=1}^{n} \frac{D_t}{(1+k_s)^t} + \sum_{t=1}^{\infty} \left[\frac{1}{(1+k_s)^n} \quad x \quad \frac{D_n(1+g_n)}{(k_s - g_n)} \right]$$

Note that $\dfrac{D_n(1+g_n)}{(k_s - g_n)}$ is equal to terminal end year's price

where

$\quad D_t \quad = D_0(1+g_s)^t$

$\quad g_s \quad = $ super normal growth rate

$\quad g_n \quad = $ normal growth rate

$\quad k_s \quad = $ required rate of return

$\quad D_n \quad = $ dividend at the nth period

$\quad D_t \quad = $ dividend at time t

Assume $D_0 = ₦2$, $k_s = 16\%$, $g = 20\%$. For the next three years and thereafter settle down to 8% per year indefinitely, then

$\quad D_1 \quad = \quad D_0(1+g) = 2(1.2) = 2.4$

$\quad D_2 \quad = \quad D_0(1+g)^2 = 2(1.2)^2 = 2.88$

$\quad D_3 \quad = \quad D_0(1+g)^3 = 2(1.2)^3 = 3.456$

$\quad D_4 \quad = \quad D_3(1+g) = 3.456(1.08) = 3.732$

Note that g here is the reduced dividend growth rate of 8% after the third year.

At this point, we have to determine the price at the end of the nth year (in this case, year 3).

$$P_3 = \frac{D_4}{(k_s - g)} = \frac{3.732}{0.16 - 0.08} = 46.66$$

We can now determine the P_0 thus

$$P_0 = \frac{D_1}{1+k} + \frac{D_2}{(1+k)^2} + \frac{D_3}{(1+k)^3} + \frac{P_3}{(1+k)^3}$$

$$P_0 = \frac{2.4}{1.16} + \frac{2.88}{(1.16)^2} + \frac{3.456}{(1.16)^3} + \frac{46.66}{(1.16)^3}$$

$$= 36.32$$

A situation of No Growth

$$P_0 = \frac{D_1}{1+r}$$

r represents discount rate (market capitalisation rate).

Here, we assume that the holding period is n, that is, the investor will hold his investment for n periods after which he would sell at a price denoted by P_1. The proceeds from the sale in period n should be included in the calculation of the share price. Therefore,

$$P_0 = \sum_{t=1}^{n} \frac{D_t}{(1+r)^t} + \frac{P_n}{(1+r)^n}$$

The price of a share is made up of two cash flow streams:

(i) the present value of the stream of dividend payments and

(ii) the present value of the end-period price.

Using a numerical example

$$P_0 = 100, \quad D_1 = 5, \quad r = 10\%, \quad P_0 = \frac{D_1 + P_1}{1+r}$$

$$P_1 = \frac{D_2 + P_2}{1+r} = \frac{5.5 + 121}{1 + 0.15} = \frac{126.5}{1.15} = 110$$

Now, assuming that dividend and price grow at a constant rate of 10% per annum:

$$P_0 = \frac{D_0}{(1+r)} + \frac{D_1 + P_2}{(1+r)^2} = \frac{5}{(1+0.15)} + \frac{5.5 + 121}{(1+0.15)^2}$$

As the horizon recedes further into the future, the present value of the end-of-period price will become so negligible that it can be ignored, whereas the cumulative value of the dividends increases and forms a layer component of share value. Hence, for an infinite period, the value of a share is simply the present value of the infinite streams of dividend payments.

Assume a constant growth

Suppose Mobil Plc has just paid a cash dividend of ₦2 per share. Investors require a 16 percent return from investment such as this. If the dividend is expected to grow at a steady 8 percent per year, what is the current value of the stock? What will the stock be worth in five years?.

The current value of the stock is:

$$P_0 = ₦2/(0.16 - 0.08) = 25$$

Price in year 5 will be determined by the dividend payment in year 6 and thereafter. As such,

$$
\begin{aligned}
P_5 &= D_6/(r - g) \\
&= D_0(1+g)^5 \\
&= 2(1+0.08)^5 \\
&= 2.9386/(r-g) \\
&= 2.9386/0.08 \\
&= 36.73
\end{aligned}
$$

Efficient Market Hypothesis

From the literature review analysis of securities pricing, three distinct schools of thought are noticeable and their views are expressed below:

Fundamentalist View

This view believes that it is the equality of the price of a security and the discounted cash flow of income from the securities that should determine the price. This translates into the fact that earnings, dividends, assets, values, quality of management returns and expected capitalisation are all important variables in the determination of the value of securities. It postulates that the analysis of economic and financial variables can be used to determine the value of securities.

The Technician's View

This school of thought is of the opinion that the forces of demand and supply determine the value of securities.

$$Ps = f(Ds, Ss)$$

Where

Ps = Price of security

Ds = Demand for security

Ss = Supply of security

f = Functional notation

This is the opinion that earnings and dividends have no influence on price-determination. It believes there is a particular common pattern that is cyclical in nature and this is a function of information, moods, guesses and opinions, which usually lead to price movement.

Random-Walk Efficient Market View

This holds the view that the stock is always in equilibrium and so would be practically impossible for an investor to consistently beat the market.

However, the market efficiency may be viewed from these perspectives:

(a)   The weak form; states that the current market price is a reflection of past price movements. Thus, paying little or no importance to today's price as a guide for determining market price.

(b)   The semi-strong form; holds the view that the current market price is a function of all publicly available information and as such market prices would have adjusted to any (good or bad) information/news as in annual reports, published data and so on.

(c)   The strong form; holds the view that current market prices reflect all information whether publicly available or privately held. This view allows "insiders" to make abnormal profit.

Apart from these three conventional forms, there equally exists the extra-sensory perspective form, holding the view that the pricing of securities has to do with the regulatory authority. This is probably the reason why some Exchanges make it publicly known that they are not behind determination of price of securities. This is evidenced in the statement of the London Stock Exchange that: "it is fundamental error to assume that the Stock Exchange 'fixes' the price of securities in which it deals".

Given the above fundamental analysis of the schools of thought existing as regards the pricing of securities in the secondary market, it could be said that the combination of ideas of each view indeed determines the price of securities in the secondary market. In other words, factors in session include:

(1) *Demand and supply and prices:* Demand and supply of a

good affects its price; if one exceeds the other, it leads to price movement and in turn price of a good equally affects its demand and supply; thus,

$$Q(d\&s) = f(P) \quad \text{and} \quad P = g(Q)$$

(2) *Expected returns on securities:* Despite the fact that the quantity of stocks an investor demands for can be partly determined by the price of the securities, there could however be an exception in which case as price increases, the investor demands for more, either to gain capital appreciation or get anticipated dividend. This, no doubt, will affect price.

(3) *Economic situation:* A politically stable economy or otherwise, doom or boom period, policy being run by the government (tight or easy); all do affect the demand and supply of securities which in turn affect the price.

(4) *Interrelationship and interdependency factors:* Production system of a company/industry in terms of technology, advertisement, etc., can change; this could in turn affect the level of profitability and in turn the demand for the company's securities. However, this is seen as a function of competence, innovativeness and extra efforts on the part of the management in taking decisions that propel the company to greater heights, above its competitors.

(5) *Information availability:* Necessary for the survival of any existing company, is the availability of the right information at the right time and at a reasonable cost which in turn is used for market advantage. Also relevant is the dissemination of information on the part of the company, as regards its performance, to the public at large and the shareholders in particular to acquaint them with happenings and decisions taken to maximise investors' interest.

(6) *Exceptional factors:* This relates to the buying of securities at any given price based on management in which there is invested interest.

(7) *Regulation on the part of institutional authority:* Prices are often regulated by an appropriate regulatory authority as in the case of;

    (a) Price Movement Suspension: when a company intends raising money (either to consolidate or diversify) from the Capital Market and submits its proposal for Public Issue to the Nigerian Stock Exchange, the security's price is made stagnant at the day's ruling price until the Issue is concluded. Trading in such securities could even be suspended to reduce speculation in the share's price in the event of any major crisis. This is equally applicable in the case of merger and acquisition and privatisation of Government-owned enterprises.

    (b) Daily Price Movement Limit: sequel to the 1997 global market collapse, members of the International Federation of Stock Exchange (FIBV) and its controlling unit (as in Security Exchange Commission in Nigeria) agreed that the volatility of the Capital Market be reduced by limiting the daily price movement. For instance with the Nigerian Stock Exchange there could only be maximum movement of 5% (upward or downward) in the price of security in a given trading day.

Conclusion

In this chapter, we discussed the important role price plays in the life and movement of any commodity or good, including securities. However, the determination of price has debatable sources, thus, making one to either believe whether "the Beast of East or West is best".

For purposes of efficiency, there must be a price attached to anything to be sold or brought, this price should be optimally determined whereby it is not overpriced or under-priced as the implication of either is obvious.

Finally, it is evident that what determines an efficient price of a stock is not a univariable factor but multivariable factors.

Some of these multivariables that could determine the price are:

    (a) The concept of demand and supply

    (b) The concept of dividend (with its history)

    (c) Results (in terms of authenticity and timeliness)

    (d) Earnings

    (e) Dissemination of information

    (f) Operating performance via quality of management

    (g) Superb Research Work on the part of Capital Market Operators especially stockbroking firms.

Chapter Nine

Mobilisation and Utilisation of Resources: The Role of the Corporate Finance Officer*

Introduction

The three "ms" of management theory are man, money and materials. The scope of our discussion in this chapter will be limited to money which, in a broad sense, can be described as "financial resources". Our main focus is on the role of the Corporate Finance Officer. A Corporate Finance Officer hoping to succeed in the ever-evolving financial markets must seek for optimum financial product mix. He should therefore be well familiar with the fundamentals of pricing as well as risk analysis in the money, capital and foreign exchange markets.

Financial Resources

In mobilising financial resources for his organisation to acquire assets to operate, a Corporate Finance Officer may consider the following options: internally generated funds (reserves), equity (money to be provided by the owners of the business), direct bank lending or other money market instruments, and long-term debt instruments from the capital market (debentures or industrial loan stock). The pecking order theory of finance advanced by Donaldson (1961) states that:

Paper Presented at the Nigerian Stock Exchange Capital Market Seminar in Akure, Ondo State on 14th November, 1996.

> Firms always preferred internal to external finance, and if they
> had to resort to external finance they would prefer to use debt,
> and only in the end equity finance.

The asset needs of a company may be financed by either the owners of the company through equity or reserves of the company or by third parties (creditors). There are two categories of the latter *viz*: Trade and Sundry creditors otherwise referred to as spontaneous financing and loan or debt which can either be short or long-term. The characteristics of trade credits are such that they are interest- free, short-term, but revolving, and they are largely driven by the level of operations of a company. Loans or debts on the other hand, are interest-bearing, their need is usually driven by the gap between the total assets of a company and its equity, plus spontaneous financing (trade credits). The availability of loan or debt depends on the willingness and comfort of the lenders to provide funding. A typical balance sheet of a corporate entity will present current assets as being financed by trade credits and short-term debts, while long-term assets are financed by long-term debts, equity and reserves. Debt is often used to refer to long-term liabilities while short - term liabilities are often referred to in specific names, such as overdraft, commercial paper, etc. However, for our purpose; both short and long-term liabilities are debts. The combination of both debt and equity is referred to as capital structure in financial management.

Characteristics of Different Types of Financial Resources

These debt obligations are usually referred to as debentures (corporate) or bonds (State or Local governments). A debenture is a security that is basically an "IOU" from the Issuer. It carries no corporate ownership privileges. They are interest-bearing obligations of companies or governments and they pay fixed periodic interest.

The return on equity is by way of dividend and price appreciation or capital gain. The dividend payment is not mandatory except the business makes profit and its directors consider such payment. Unlike debt, repayment of the principal is very rare except where a company is quoted on the Stock Exchange, whereby its stocks can easily be traded through secondary dealing. Even in such a case, the company is not the one directly repaying the principal. The shares only change hands. Equity cannot be withdrawn at the contributor's option, while return is unlimited but depends on the profitability of the business. Holders of equity have the lowest priority for the repayment in the event of liquidation of a company. Hence, they bear the residual risk.

The common types of equity are ordinary shares and preference shares. The holders of ordinary shares have unlimited interest in the residual profit or loss of their company. They get their return in the form of dividend from the after tax profit. They also derive capital gains on the value of their shares. The holders of ordinary shares have voting rights and therefore determine who is elected to the board of their company. They can increase their stakes in the company through fresh issue of shares either for cash or through bonus issue or rights issues.

Preference shares, on the other hand are hybrid of debt and equity. The fixed nature of the dividend gives the instrument the character of debt while the irredeemable feature confers on it an equity status.

Dividend is paid to the holders of preference shares as an appropriation of profits. Holders of preference shares take priority in dividend payment over ordinary shareholders. They receive payment after debt instrument holders, but before ordinary shareholders upon liquidation. There are several variations of preference shares *viz*, redeemable or irredeemable, fixed or floating dividend, cumulative, participative, etc. Redeemable preference shares may be classified as debt or equity depending on substance.

Long and Short-Term Finance

The distinction between long-term and short-term finance is that whereas the former is contractually available for several years and hence very stable, the latter is contractually available for a short period hence upon its maturity, the funding has to be replaced with another or similar funding such as trade credits. Funding a business with long or undated tenure involved the use of long-term debt of over five years maturity, and equity provided by the owners of the business.

The foregoing distinction between long-term and short-term finance has important implications for proper finance management, and so a good Corporate Finance Officer must apply his professional skill in the choice of the various sources of funding his organisation's activities. Ideally, long-term assets should be financed by long-term funds whereas short-term assets should be financed by either short or long-term funds.

Types of Short-Term Debt

Short-term debts comprise Bank Overdraft, Trade Credits, Commercial Papers and Bankers' Acceptances.

Bank Overdraft

Bank overdraft is the facility which is provided by clearing–banks to their customers to overdraw their accounts to specified limits. The balance on account usually fluctuates, but the upper limit cannot be exceeded. Interest is payable on the outstanding balance, and the amount is repayable on demand, hence an overdraft facility is short-term in nature. Such facility is however renewable. Companies often make use of this form of financing to bridge the short-term gap between their earnings and expenditures. Bank overdraft facility can be used to pay salaries and meet immediate pressing obligations. The cost of this facility varies from bank to bank, but it is usually in line with the interest rate regime in the economy. Overdraft facility may not be appropriate for financing long-term projects.

Trade Credits

Trade credits, otherwise called spontaneous finance, are the funding provided by the company's suppliers, and they are usually self-replacing. A wise Corporate Finance Officer will always explore the use of this form of interest-free credit. Trade credit requires the supplier of required items for a company's operation to supply in advance over a period after which payment will be made.

Commercial Papers

Other means by which a company can be financed on short-term basis is the use of Commercial Papers. This is a paper evidencing a debt owed by a company to a lender. It is used mainly by blue chip companies whose financial worth is attractive to the lender. The Commercial paper is usually arranged, and may be guaranteed by a bank. The major characteristic of a Commercial Paper is that the borrower receives money lower than the face value since interest payable is deducted upfront, that is, the paper is discounted. The effective interest rate is higher than the discount rate.

Bankers' Acceptance

Bankers' Acceptance is the Commercial Paper of a bank, that is, the bank accepts the bill. Technically, the accepting bank is the primary obligor rather than the borrowing party. Bankers' Acceptance is usually used to facilitate trade, especially international trade. This form of short-term financing is mainly attractive to the quoted companies because of the off-balance sheet way it is accounted for, hence it has a tax advantage.

Types of Long-Term Debt

The variants of long-term debt are Leases, Term Loan, and Debentures.

Leases

Leases are usually used to finance specific fixed asset acquisitions. Leasing is an arrangement whereby the owner of an asset (the lessor) transfers the use of the asset to the prospective or current user of that asset (the lessee) for a period of time, which is usually less than the asset's economic life. In consideration for the use of the asset, the lessee compensates the lessor by paying rent, and after the expiration of the lease period as contained in an agreement, the lessee returns the asset to the lessor. In finance lease, the ownership can be transferred to the lessee on the payment of a purchase option equal to the residual value of the asset.

Leasing arrangement are generally based on the belief that it is the use to which an asset is put that is important rather than the ownership of that asset. This is an important factor to consider by a Corporate Finance Officer in mobilising and utilising resources for his organisation. Leasing has assumed an increasing importance as a mode of financing the acquisition and use of fixed assets, ranging from copiers and motor vehicles to manufacturing plants and other highly expensive and easily-turned-obsolete capital equipment in this ever-changing technological world.

Leasing is a flexible financing tool which meets the different needs of companies. For example, a young start-up company may lease equipment to conserve cash or as a means of avoiding the often strict collateral requirement which a bank loan may require. Blue chip companies make use of leasing arrangement to acquire equipment thus keeping bank credit lines free for other purposes. It is pertinent to note also that leasing has tax implications for both the lessee and the lessor. The two major types of leases are Finance Lease and Operating Lease.

Term Loan

Term loan has a long repayment tenure of over five years. There is always a periodic repayment of both the interest and capital. A term loan may or may not be project-related. However, where it is project-related it is described as 'Project Finance'. The loan may be secured or unsecured. Only companies with good trade records with a bank can obtain an unsecured term loan from such a bank. In such circumstances negative pledge is made. A term loan is usually sought by a company to finance an asset with long gestation period and the returns on such asset spread into the future.

Debenture.

Debenture is a document evidencing indebtedness under seal, stating provisions on interest payments and principal repayments. Debenture may be unsecured or secured. The terms are usually stated in the underlying agreement schedule, interest charges, information to be provided, fee payable, and borrower's "negative" covenants. Holders of secured debenture rank only after the company's trade creditors for repayment as the underlying assets are sold in the event of the issuing company being wound up. The rating of a debenture stock will reflect to some extent the status of the issuing company. Unlike loan which is arranged through a bank, debenture is a Capital Market instrument which is packaged by an Issuing House.

Capital Market

The Capital Market constitutes the cheapest source of mobilisation of long-term resources for existing projects, working capital, expansion programme and capital formation.

Since the Nigerian Stock Exchange (NSE) was established, a total of 275 securities, made up of 30 Government stocks, 62 industrial loan (debenture preference stock) and 183 ordinary shares of firms had been listed for trading on the floors of the Exchange.

There are many ways firms can raise fund through the Capital Market. Some of these are discussed below.

Private Placement

Though the private placement of securities, has the undertone of Capital Market activities, its process has little to do with the Stock Exchange and/or some of its other agencies. Unlike other forms of securities issue done with the approval of Securities and Exchange Commission (SEC) and the NSE, private issues involve placement of equities/shares of company (ies), mainly limited liability firms to selected number of investors. A private enterprise could issue its shares, as a means of raising funds for expansion programmes, etc, to selected but trusted individuals.

The shares so issued are not listed on the Stock Exchange, so they do not qualify for trading on the floor of The Exchange. Nevertheless, they represent one of the cheapest sources of funding small and medium scale enterprises.

Rights Issue

Many companies quoted on the NSE continue to utilise this means to get additional funds needed for recapitalisation, working capital or expansion scheme. The new equities issued through this process are subscribed to by the existing shareholders of the issuing firm. Rights Issue are distributed to shareholders in proportion to their existing holdings and such shares are bought at less than the current market price.

Offer for Subscription or Public Issue

Companies intending to be listed on the Stock Exchange usually issue their new shares to the public at price approved by SEC. New ordinary shares are also made available to the public by existing quoted companies. Proceeds from the offers are utilised to refinance debt, refurbish or replace obsolete plants and machinery and also for expansion programme as the case may be. The procedure for embarking on public offer is usually long, as the approval of regulatory authorities must be sought and obtained and the extra-ordinary general meeting of shareholders must give its nod to the Public Issue.

Debenture Stocks/Bond

As earlier explained in this paper, debenture represents a promise by a company to pay back certain amount of loan raised through the Capital Market at a fixed interest rate.

Utilisation of Financial Resources

In optimally utilising the available resources in the Financial Markets, a Corporate Finance Officer must put into focus what he considers the desirable capital structure of his company. Capital structure measures the relative magnitude of debt versus equity capital employed to finance the company. This is often referred to as gearing. This relation has a major impact on two key issues *viz*: financial risk and cost of capital.

Financial Risk

A company faces many business risks but financial risk specifically relates to the presence of a debt in a company's capital structure. Debt requires certain financial obligations including repayment of interest and the principal when due. The inability to meet these cash obligations as at when due constitutes a risk. This risk may or may not crystallise depending on the ability of the company to generate sufficient cash to meet debt obligations. As debt increases, risk to equity shareholders and new holders of debt instrument increase. The interest rate on new debt increases and the expectation of return by equity shareholders will also increase.

In the light of the foregoing, the optimal capital structure which a good Corporate Finance Officer should strive to achieve is the one which maximises the value of the company. Many financial management books contain theories on how to determine the optimum capital structure, but facts also exist in practice which limit the level of debt a company should go for.

In spite of risk associated with debt, a Corporate Finance Officer can still take advantage of debt financing where the potential of earnings from the utilisation of borrowed funds are greater than interest cost. Also, cost of debt may be lower than equity especially after tax. It is instructive to note also that interest expenses are tax deductible unlike dividends. One other important advantage of using debt is that where economic distortions are present, such as we have in Nigeria, cost of debt may be negative, that is, below the inflation rate and therefore very cheap.

Cost of Capital

The second factor to be considered in arriving at optimum capital structure is the cost of capital. This is the rate of return that must be earned on new investment with the same average risk as the firm's existing assets, in order to provide the firm with fair market rates of return. The application of the concept of opportunity cost of capital

(WACC) used by a company consists of risk free rate of return, premium for business risk, and premium for financial risk. The WACC is that rate used in investment appraisal. The formulae for calculating both the cost of debt and cost of equity are as follows:

Cost of Debt

(i)   Without Flotation Costs

The after-tax cost of debt is the before-tax cost multiplied by one, minus the marginal corporate tax rate (T). Thus, $K_d = \dfrac{r_d(1-T)}{D}$

Where

K_d – After tax cost of debt

r_d – Before-tax cost of Debt

T – Tax Rate

D – Market Value of Debt

- Tax shield effect is only applicable to companies susceptible to taxation

(ii)   With Flotation Cost

$$K_d = \frac{r_d(1-T)}{1-f_d}$$

Where f_d is the % flotation cost

Cost of Equity

Expected rate of return by ordinary shareholders.

Constant Growth Model

(i)   Without Flotation Costs:

$$K_e = \frac{D}{MV} + g$$

Where

D   – dividend to be paid into the foreseeable future (sustainable dividend)

MV   – market value of share

g   – expected growth rate (constant)

(ii)   With Flotation Cost:

$$K_e = \frac{D}{MV(1 - f_e)} + g$$

Cost of Retained Earnings

Using the Constant-Growth Model with the expected cash dividend one year from now, the current market price, MV and a constant growth rate, g, the cost of retained earnings is

$$K_s = \frac{D_1}{MV} + g$$

Cost of Preferred Shares

(i)   Without Flotation Costs:

$$K_p = \frac{D_p}{P_p}$$

Where

D_p is the cash dividend per share on preferred stock

P_p, the market value of preferred stock.

(ii)   With Flotation Costs:

$$K_p = \frac{D_p}{P_p(1 - f_p)}$$

Cost of equity using Capital Asset Pricing Model (CAPM)

$$K_e = R_f + \beta_e\{ E(R_m) - R_f \}$$

Where β_e is the beta coefficient of the stock, R_f is the risk free rate, and $E(R_m)$ is the expected return on the market portfolio. The beta measures the degree of responsiveness of the stock's return to the market return.

The Weighted Average Cost of Capital

The cost of generating capital for investment activity by the firm, is given by the Weighted Average Cost of Capital:

$$\text{WACC} = w\,k_d + w\,k_e + w\,k_s + w\,k_p$$

$$\text{or WACC} = k_d(D/V) + k_e(E/V) + k_p(P/V) + k_s(R/V)$$

Where w_s is the weight or proportion of each source of finance to the total finance. The weights should be based on market values.

Conclusion

In mobilising and utilising financial resources, a Corporate Finance Officer should analyse the financing needs of his organisation. Such analysis will be driven by the required asset level for operations, desired capital structure, level of spontaneous financing available and the extent of seasonality of the underlying business. The asset level is a function of the expected business volume or turnover, capital expenditures, input and sales prices (allowing for inflation), level of stocking, credit sales policy, cash holding requirement, other asset levels, trade credit policies, and seasonality considerations. The funding requirement of the asset level will take into consideration the use of both the long-term and short-term finance. The desired debt/equity structure and the availability of debt at desired level will be determined by the company's policies, the lenders' willingness to lend to the company as well as the company's borrowing capacity.

Under the present economic circumstances, a good Corporate Finance Officer should be more circumspect in using bank facilities such as overdraft and bank loans in funding medium and long-term programmes, despite the prevailing fall in the interest rate due to sudden improvement on liquidity in the system. The prevailing 'excess' liquidity in the banking sector was due mainly to the injection of a substantial part of the Petroleum Trust Fund (PTF) resources into the system and the refund of the stabilisation securities holdings of some banks hitherto held by the Central Bank of Nigeria (CBN). These sources of funds are temporary in nature and can dry up soon, thereby creating another fund liquidity squeeze in the system that may eventually affect the interest rate movement. One must be able to look beyond the immediate economic horizon and project ahead on the implications of present action on the future of the organisation.

Finally, much as the macro-economic environment has recorded some measure of stability in the last few months, one should not foreclose the possibility of a reversal in policy against the backdrop of previous experience. Equally, the promulgation of two investment decrees: Investment Promotion Decree 6 of 1995 and Foreign Exchange Monitoring Decree 17 of 1995, should be seen as a challenge in looking beyond the shores of this country in sourcing for fresh foreign capital either as equity holding or debenture to finance the projects of corporate entities in Nigeria.

Chapter Ten

Privatisation of Public Enterprises in Nigeria: Objectives, Strategies, Challenges and Prospects*

What is Privatisation?

Privatisation involves redefining the role of the State by disengaging it from those activities which are best done by the private sector. The objective is to achieve economic efficiency for the greater benefit of the entire society. There is no doubt that privatisation is a political process which has to be accomplished through economic exercise. Privatisation may take either the form of non-divestiture or divestiture. The first may be a step to the second.

Non-divestiture options, can help to create the necessary political will as well as advance the privatisation process by demonstrating the commercial viability of public enterprises. They may serve as important measures in themselves or as preparatory steps to divestiture. Such options include:

i.   Management privatisation, including management contracts, leasing and operating concessions;

ii.   Restructuring and commercialisation or corporatisation, to be combined with management privatisation, as desired or necessary; and

---

Paper Presented at Capital Market Correspondents Association of Nigeria Forum, held in Lagos, December 1999.

iii.   Contracting out public services.

Divestiture options include:

i.   Direct sale, full or partial, to general investors;

ii.   Private placement with "strategic" investors or to joint venture partners;

iii.   Public share offerings on Stock Markets (usually for profitable, large-scale public enterprises);

iv.   Public auctions (usually for small or medium-sized public enterprises which do not require technology transfer);

v.   Sale to employees or management teams through employee share ownership plans, management or employee buy-outs ("internal privatisations").

vi.   Sale to investment or mutual funds;

vii.   Mass privatisation; and

viii. Liquidation, followed by the sale of assets (where the latter can fetch a higher price than the sale of the entire enterprise or where it may be necessary because of excessive strain on the budget).

The concept of privatisation is not new in Nigeria. Indeed, it was put to practice within the larger framework of Structural Adjustment Programme in Nigeria between 1988 and 1993. However, since 1993, there has been a lingering lull in the privatisation programme. This loss of steam does not derive from a loss of faith in the restructuring of the programme or that it had become politically unfashionable. It is rather traceable to the introduction of intricate economic and political variables into the matrix of the programme. No doubt, the introduction of these pressure-exerting factors weakened Government's resolve to continue with the implementation of the programme and consequently the noticeable loss of speed and eventual halting of the process in 1993.

The stage has now been set for the second phase of the privatisation programme. One can only pray that the Administration of President Obasanjo will be fully committed to privatisation, to avoid the inherent dangers of vested interest and misgiving about government's intentions. Being an open economy, Nigeria is in a better situation than countries of Eastern Europe and former Soviet Union where there had been high dependence on the State for the provision of all services.

Objectives

The main objective of privatisation is to accelerate the restructuring of the Nigerian economy for sustainable growth and optimum resource utilisation. A properly conceived and well articulated privatisation programme will no doubt enhance the optimisation of government assets and free funds for national development. Privatisation is also consistent with the government policy of making the private sector the engine of growth of the Nigerian economy and the dominant contributor to the Gross Domestic Product (GDP).

Strategy

To ensure success in the execution of the ongoing privatisation programme, the following strategic steps should be taken:

(i)   Defining the broad extent of privatisation;

(ii)   Stating clearly the political, economic and social objectives to be achieved;

(iii)   Establishing clear guidelines or criteria for valuation; the choice of public enterprises for privatisation; and for the choice of buyers;

(iv)   Selecting techniques and, as necessary, the sequence appropriate to the policy objectives to be attained and the needs of the public enterprises to be privatised; creating confidence in the process, for example by starting with privatisations with a high prospect of success; promoting effective corporate governance, for example through the participation of "core" investors;

(v) Ensuring transparency and accountability in the privatisation process and using competitive bidding to the fullest extent possible;

(vi) Mounting a programme to promote public awareness of the value of privatisation to the economy so as to contribute to the building up of broad-based consensus;

(vii) Building marketing upfront in each privatisation operation to stimulate potential interest among investors and thus enhance the value of the public enterprise to be privatised, remembering that, apart from "small privatisations", no two privatisations are the same;

(viii) Promoting popular participation in the privatisation process through the allocation of a proportion of corporation shares to small investors ("popular capitalism") or through mass privatisation;

(ix) Addressing the concerns of employees by paying particular attention to their acquired rights, compensation measures for retrenched workers and to employment protection and job creation measures;

(x) Promoting employee participation in the privatisation process through the allocation of a proportion of corporate shares, as reflected in the special provision of 10% equity to employees of the privatised entity;

(xi) Addressing the concerns of consumers through appropriate regulation of privatised monopolies and machinery to handle consumer complaints;

(xii) Taking steps, for example, by specifying conditions in sales agreements, to prevent abuses such as unauthorised transfers to third parties of privatised enterprises immediately after their divestiture.

(xiii) Defining the role of foreign participation with regard to large-scale or strategic enterprises

(xiv) Providing for safeguards (such as the use of "golden share") in strategic enterprises in order, for example, to prevent hostile takeovers; and

(xv) Establishing mechanism or procedures for monitoring the progress and results of privatisation, including compliance with commitments made by private investors.

Challenges

The four challenges that must be addressed in the second phase of privatisation are as follows:

1.   How to ensure proper planning;

2.   How to put proper organisational structures in place;

3.   How to ensure widespread participation; and

4.   How to finance the privatisation.

These issues are considered in detail in the sections following.

Planning

The initial planning required is to plan for the success of the privatisation programme itself. This is the key to creating the necessary credibility for the programme in the future. An unplanned or unsuccessful privatisation activity involving public enterprises will create doubts in the minds of the public and will lead to backlash of public criticisms. There is therefore wisdom in planning for success right from the outset of the privatisation programme. Proper planning can be achieved through the strategy highlighted above.

Organisation

A major step towards a successful privatisation programme is the strength of the organisational structures that are in place to implement the privatisation programme. During the first phase of privatisation in Nigeria (1988 – 1993), decisions on what to privatise, when to privatise, price of shares to be offered for sale to the public, allotment of shares of privatised enterprises, prices of assets to be sold and to whom were the sole responsibility of the Federal Executive Council, under advice from the Technical Committee on Privatisation and Commercialisation (TCPC).

The Obasanjo Administration has come up with a new body called the Privatisation Council under the Chairmanship of the Vice-President, Alhaji Abubakar Atiku. It is hoped that the body will only be charged with policy making, leaving the technical and day-to-day administrative issues of privatisation to the Bureau of Public Enterprises (BPE). In this regard, the proposed role of the Privatisation Council should include, among others;

(i)   Approving the broad policies on privatisation;

(ii) Determining the potential economic and social objectives to be achieved;

(iii) Establishing clear guidelines or criteria for valuation of public enterprises;

(iv) Approving enterprises to be privatised;

(v)   Deciding on the timing of the privatisation;

(vi) Appointing or selecting core/strategic investors.

On the other hand, it is pertinent to mention here that it is fair to suggest that since the learning curve in privatisation is usually quite long, the Bureau of Public Enterprise (BPE) should be strengthened, reorganised and empowered to continue the implementation of the programme. In order to ensure the smooth implementation of the privatisation programme, the BPE should be made accountable to the Privatisation Council which in turn will brief the President-in-Council from time to time. The Presidency should also apprise the National Assembly accordingly. Thus, akin to the case of the TCPC Decree No. 25 of 1998, the following functions among others, of the erstwhile TCPC, should be transferred automatically to the BPE:

(a) Advising on the capital restructuring needs of the enterprises to be privatised or commercialised to ensure a good market reception for those to be privatised, as well as to facilitate their good management and independent access to the Capital Market:

(b) Carrying out all activities required for the successful public issue of the shares of the enterprises to be privatised, including the appointment of Issuing Houses, Stockbrokers, Solicitors, Trustees, Accountants and other professionals to the issue;

(c) Advising the Privatisation Council after consultation with the Securities and Exchange Commission (SEC) and Nigerian Stock Exchange (NSE) on the allotment pattern for the sale of the shares by the enterprises concerned.

(d) Overseeing the actual sale of the shares of the affected enterprises by the Issuing Houses, in accordance with the guidelines approved by the Federal Government;

(e) Submitting to the Privatisation Council from time to time, for the purpose of approval, proposals on the sale of government shares in the affected enterprises, with a view to ensuring a fair price and even spread in the ownership of the shares.

(f) Ensuring the success of the privatisation and commercialisation exercise, taking into account the need for balanced and meaningful participation by Nigerians and foreigners in accordance with the relevant Nigerian laws;

(g) Ensuring the up-dating of the accounts of all affected enterprises with a view to ensuring financial discipline.

Widespread Participation

Many governments have incorporated social provisions and other support measures in their privatisation programmes, reflecting the importance which they attach to social objectives in the privatisation process. The main areas which should be covered to ensure mass participation are:

(a) Providing sources of funds for shares acquisition;

(b) Ensuring employment protection and the safeguarding of employees' rights and benefits;

(c) Ensuring preferential allocation for shares to employees and small investors;

(d) Providing timely and accurate information on enterprises for privatisation;

(e) Ensuring flexible channels for distribution of documents and information;

(f) Aiding small investors to pay for shares instalmentally;

(g) Creating a Special Trust for weaker sections of the society. The Special Trust Fund will purchase the shares of this group of people in Trust for them until they are in a position to buy back their shares;

(h) Determining the level of foreign participation;

(i) Encouraging Nigerians living abroad to invest in privatisation enterprises;

(j) Utilising the proceeds of privatisation to finance industrial, human resources and infrastructural development; and

(k) Embarking on public awareness campaigns in the media to create widespread support for the privatisation programme.

Financing

Finance poses a great challenge to the success of privatisation in many developing countries, including Nigeria. With global financial resources being stretched by the demand from other developing countries and the industrialising countries of Asia, and given the large number of attractive projects in other countries, the need to clearly map out the means of financing the privatisation exercise becomes glaring and inescapable. There is therefore a need to:

(a) identify sources of funds for purchasing public enterprises in order to determine the techniques and timing of sales and the success of such sales;

(b) strengthen financial institutions and markets, including both formal and informal networks of financial intermediation;

(c) structure the privatisation exercise properly to effectively tap domestic savings and attract foreign investment.

The major financing models used in the last privatisation and commercialisation programme in Nigeria, which will be relevant in the forthcoming exercise include:

1. Public share offerings on the Nigerian Stock Exchange.

2. Domestic entrepreneurs and institutional investors, including banks, insurance companies and pension funds were a veritable source.

3. Privatised companies and other companies which were urged to give share loans to their employees in order to purchase shares of the privatised enterprises.

4. Foreign participation in the privatisation exercise was allowed by the TCPC Decree No. 25 of 1988.

5. Buying in trust by State Investment Corporations for citizens of each State, where shares were warehoused only for the State's citizens until such a time the citizens were well placed to buy the shares of the State, when investor demand had increased. In some countries, e.g. Malaysia, special Privatisation Trust Funds (PTF) were established to 'warehouse' minority shares in public enterprises. Privatisation Trust Fund (PTF) can remove a large chunk of shares from direct government control and enable the public to participate in their sale in the future after the PTFs have consolidated their portfolios of privatised enterprises.

Prospects

There is no doubt that the second phase of the privatisation programme has a brighter prospect as the programme will be more comprehensive in depth and coverage than the first phase. This time around, large, capital intensive and basic industries such as paper and steel mills, sugar companies, fertilizer companies and vehicle assembly plants will be privatized either totally or partially. Many public utilities such as NITEL and NEPA are slated for privatisation. The implication of this is that proceeds from privatisation will be enormous, hence the capacity of the Nigerian Capital Market to absorb this volume will be put to test. The institutional capacity of the Nigerian Capital Market must therefore be strengthened. Cross border listing of shares is another veritable means of accommodating the octopus privatisation.

Privatisation, is not merely desirable, it is altogether necessary. It will not solve all macro-economic problems hindering the realisation of an adequate growth rate and the restructuring of the Nigerian economy, but it will prevent the nation from the certain disaster that results from perennial public sector inefficiencies. Planned privatisation has the capacity to unleash diversified sectoral growth through an optimal process of resources reallocation and factor redeployment. In Nigeria's case, government divestiture from certain public entities will open up tremendous possibilities for increased and more efficient delivery of goods and services at affordable prices, higher and more efficient employment and improved living standards.

The current high "real" price of electricity, water, telecommunications, transportation, and petroleum products contribute greatly to Nigeria's high and uncompetitive cost of domestic production. Privatising these enterprises on a feasible phased plan will create the possibilities for long-term least cost of production and, ultimately, realign Nigeria's competitiveness internationally over a large range of goods and services, via the input-output matrix. This will also induce higher capital flows across the entire economy through linkages with various sub-sectors.

Chapter Eleven

Potential Impact of the 1999 Federal Government Budget on the Nigerian Capital Market*

Introduction

The Nigerian economy has witnessed some elements of deregulation in the recent past. This, ostensibly, was to create a conducive economic environment to enhance growth and development. However, the structural problems and constraints in the system have not allowed the desired impact to be felt. The policies and programmes raised in the 1999 budget were aimed at tackling these structural problems and removing the constraints.

In the light of the foregoing, broad objectives of the 1999 Federal Budget were as follows:

(i) "to expand the existing revenue base by exploring new sources;

(ii) to improve internal security to create a safe environment for the pursuit of economic and social activities;

(iii) to continue with the policy of privatisation of State-owned enterprises;

(iv) to eliminate the dual exchange rate regime;

Paper Presented at the Seminar organised by the Finance Correspondents Association of Nigeria held in January, 1999.

167

(v)   to maintain appropriate fiscal, monetary and exchange rate policies with a view to achieving overall macro-economic stability;

(vi)   to sustain prudent internal and external debt management;

(vii) to enhance efforts in capacity building and utilisation;

(viii) to reduce the level of unemployment;

(ix)   to improve the purchasing power of the citizenry;

(x)   to sustain the single digit inflation rate achieved in the 1998 financial year; and

(xi)   to achieve at least 3% overall growth rate of the GDP".

Among the strategies designed to achieve the foregoing objectives, the two that are very germane to the development of the capital market are the acceleration of the privatisation of state-owned enterprises, economic liberalisation and competition processes, as well as the continuation of the battle against ills of the society such as "advance fee fraud", money laundering and similar vices which have given Nigeria a negative image.

1998 Stock Market Performance

It is pertinent to compare stock market performance in 1998 with 1997 in order to provide a projection for 1999 based on the policies and objectives of the 1999 budget. The following statistics serve as a useful tool for analysis:

Table 8.1 Statistical Summary of Stock Market Performance

	1998	1997
Volume	2.1bn	1.3bn
Value (₦)	13.5bn	1.1bn
New Issue approval (₦)	16.4bn	7.6bn
Foreign Portfolio transactions ($)	49.7m	9.4bn
The NSE all-share index	5672.76	6440.51
Market capitalisation (₦)	263.3bn	292.9bn
Average P/E ratio	11.2	11.9
No of listed companies	186	182

*Source: The Nigerian Stock Exchange Report from *Policy Magazine* Vol. 4, No. 2 Jan. 11-17, 1999.

The above statistics show that while the volume of transactions and value in Naira term increased between 1997 and 1998, the all-share index and total market capitalisation declined, so also did the average price-earning ratio. Although the value of the new Issues approved by both the Securities and Exchange Commission (SEC) and the Nigerian Stock Exchange (NSE) increased by over 100% between the two years, the number of companies listed on the Nigerian Stock Exchange increased by four only. This may be due to two factors.

One, many of the companies, which raised capital through public offerings, were already quoted on the Stock Exchange. Two, the astronomical increase in the value of the issues, may be due to the large volume of issues brought to the market by one or two of the new issues notably, the Nigerian Energy Sector Fund (NESF) issued by NAL Merchant Bank Plc in 1988. On the other hand, the reason for the decline in the all-price index and market capitalisation in 1998 was as a result of poor corporate performance and declining share prices, throughout that year.

The analysis above suggests that although the 1998 budget

contained far reaching policy measures which could have improved the capital market fortunes, most of these measures, which were derived from the recommendations of the Vision 2010 Report, were not implemented. This has been the bane of economic development in Nigeria. Nigerians are very good at generating good ideas, but very poor at implementing them.

Other factors, which accounted for poor performance of the capital market in 1998 were exogenous and these included:

(1) decline in the price of oil and

(2) the South East Asian crisis.

From the domestic front, lack of transparency in the economic system as well as the energy and political crisis militated against the achievement of set objectives for the economy in general and the capital market in particular.

Federal Government Budget: Problems and Prospects for the Nigerian Capital Market

The editorial of the *Policy Magazine* of January 11–17, 1999, describes the budget in the following terms:

> There is nothing new in the budget. Many of the things which they have said this year we've heard last year or years past. We can only appeal to them to try and implement them.

This is an apt description of the Nigerian Budgetary Policy. If only Government will implement the 1999 budget, the impact on the capital market will begin to be felt by the first quarter of this year.

However, it will be naive to assume that the implementation of some of the measures contained in the budget will not adversely affect prospective investors. Such measures include the very conservative low government revenue projection and the attendant tight spending plan, the increase in petroleum products prices, the removal of some of the incentives won by the real sector of the economy in the past years, and the reduction in capital spending by the government.

In spite of the problems likely to be created by these measures highlighted, there are some measures contained in the budget which will, no doubt, have salutary effect on the capital market, if properly implemented.

The plan by government to securitise domestic debts in the course of the fiscal year is a welcome development. The securitised debts will be traded on the Nigerian Stock Exchange. The securitisation, according to the Hon. Minister of Finance, will contribute to the nation's economic recovery as well as help the distressed institutions to which many local contractors are heavily indebted.

Another important step is the plan to promulgate an enabling legislation for the formal take off of the Abuja Stock Exchange. Perhaps, it should be mentioned here that the merits of multiple Stock Exchange and the promise they hold would be put to test. The success of this new effort rests on market professionals and government. A market structure and market practices which will sustain and deepen public confidence, ensure its growth and professionalism will be required. Government, on its part, must ensure the continued enhancement of the economic structure and regulations to support stability, growth, transparency and accountability in the capital market. Multiple Exchange on their own will not create a vibrant and growing capital market; all depend, of course, on the practitioners, the regulators, and the government.

Another aspect of the 1999 budget that should have great impact on the capital market is the full implementation of the privatisation programme. Although, the budget speech of the Head of State and the press briefing by the Hon. Minister of Finance indicated that a legislation would be promulgated expeditiously to give legal backing to the privatisation programme, there is no definite time table to show how the administration intends to achieve this between then and May 29th, 1999, when it will hand over to civil administration. Such a definite programme of action will be very reassuring and it is not too late for government to come out with a timetable.

In view of the tight Federal Government Budget which leaves little room for saving and investment, the buoyancy of the Nigerian Capital Market will be influenced largely in 1999 by investment from external sources. It is in this regard that the ongoing diplomatic efforts of the present administration should continue, coupled with the continuation of the battle against ills of the society, highlighted earlier on in this chapter, which had given Nigeria a negative image in the past. These efforts will assist in attracting both direct and portfolio investments into the country.

Conclusion

The poor implementation of the 1998 Federal Government Budget among other factors, accounted for the low performance of the Capital Market that year. The prospects for the Capital Market in 1999 are bright if, and only if, the present administration is determined to accomplish the stated objectives before it hands over power in May 1999. The successful conclusion of the transition programme as well as the proper commencement of privatisation programme will both have far reaching implications for investment decisions by Nigerians and foreigners alike.

Chapter Twelve

The Investment Climate in Nigeria*
A Case for Foreign Investment in the Nigerian Wire and Cable Plc.

Introduction

Nigeria is the world's most populous black nation, with approximately 110 million people. Among them are many conscientious, hardworking people wishing and striving to shape a new course for their country in the 21st century, under a democratic environment. Endowed with vast and varied resources, Nigeria offers enormous opportunities for investment.

State of the Economy

With the return to civil rule in 1999 after sixteen years of military administration, Nigeria now enjoys macro-economic stability. However, the projected expansion of the national economy is yet to be achieved due to decline in capacity utilisation, decaying infrastructures, rising unemployment and inflation. The present Civilian Administration has put policies and programmes in place to achieve the following quantitative targets:

A Brief for Nigerian Wire and Cable Plc's Visit to South Korea, in January, 2001.

Table 14.1 Quantitative Targets for Nigeria's Economy

		Targets (2003)	1999
1.	GDP growth Rate	10%	2.4%
2.	Inflation rate	Single Digit	13%
3.	Gainfully employed labour force (both formal and informal)	70%	50%
4.	Population access to safe water	60%	40%
5.	Household access to electricity	60%	40%
6.	Functional telephone lines per 1000 persons	30%	4%
7.	Population of school-age children in school	90%	50%
8.	Literacy population level	80%	57%
9.	Nutrition level (daily calorie)	2500	2120
10.	Other basic human needs (level of satisfaction)	Medium/High	Low
11.	Reduction in child malnutrition	20% of total population of children	46% of total Population of children
12.	Infant mortality	50 per 1000 births	78 per 1000 births
13.	Maternal mortality	400 per 100,000 births	800 per 100,000 births
14.	Promotion of women's participation in informal sector, food processing and subsistence agriculture.	Recognition and inclusion in the national accounting system of the economy	Invisible

Investment Policy

The investment policy of Nigeria allows equal opportunities to domestic and foreign investors. It has opened all sectors of the economy including infrastructure, agriculture and a vast segment of the social and service sectors, to direct foreign investment. The Economic Vision recently announced, and the political and social re-engineering measures initiated by President Obasanjo's Administration have resulted in a positive improvement in the national psyche and even more so in the economy; it has accelerated the restoration of investor confidence and created the right perceptions.

The battle against corruption is real and effective as evidenced by recent events. The strengthening of the operational capability of the public service and national security units has commenced and remains on course. The recent increase in the minimum wage, though relatively marginal, has improved the purchasing power of the nation's huge market. More people are demanding for goods and services that they erstwhile could not afford. This in turn will encourage producers to increase production, increase capacity utilisation and employment.

The new policy providing liberal incentives, in particular the free choice to foreign investors to make investment up to 100% equity in new enterprises are clear indications that Nigeria's investment climate is among the most attractive and competitive in the region and must invite and encourage new investments in this growing regional market.

The Nigerian Investment Promotion Commission is evolving into a truly one-stop agency geared towards providing facilitation services to investors for the speedy realisation of their new investments and joint venture projects. The commission takes prompt action whenever required in resolving issues relating to new investment by eliminating bureaucratic impediments and other roadblocks. It is totally committed to the rapid growth and development of the private sector and the economy as a whole.

The Nigerian Capital Market

The Nigerian Stock Exchange was established in 1960 as the Lagos Stock Exchange. In December 1977, it became The Nigerian Stock Exchange, with branches established in some of the major commercial cities of the country. At present, there are six branches of The Nigerian Stock Exchange, each with a trading floor.

The Exchange started operations in Lagos in 1961 with 19 securities listed for trading. Today there are 266 securities listed on The Exchange, made up of 17 Government stocks, 53 industrial loan (debenture/preference) stocks and 196 equity/ordinary shares of companies, all with a total market capitalisation of approximately ₦366.9 billion.

Most of the listed companies have foreign/multinational affiliations and represent a cross-section of the economy, ranging from agriculture through manufacturing to services.

The Nigerian Capital Market has in place a tested network of Stockbroking firms, Issuing Houses, merchant banks, corporate law firms and over 50 quality firms of auditors and reporting accountants [most with international link.]

The Stock Exchange and most of the nation's stockbroking firms and Issuing Houses are staffed with creative financial engineers that can compete anywhere in the world. The market has in place a network of intermediating organisations that can effectively and creditably meet the challenges and growing needs of investors in Nigeria.

Integrity is the watchword of The Stock Exchange. Market operators subscribe to the code "Our word is our bond". Thus, public trust in the Nigerian Stock Market has grown tremendously, with about three million individual investors and hundreds of institutional investors (including foreigners who own about 47% of the quoted companies) using the facilities of The Exchange. The Stock Exchange's 40 years history is devoid of any fraud, shocks, scandals or insider dealings.

Trading

The Nigerian Stock Exchange has been operating an Automated Trading System (ATS) since April 27, 1999, with dealers trading through a network of computers connected to a server.

The ATS has facility for remote trading and surveillance. Consequently, the Abuja Area office of The Exchange is connected for online real time trading. The Exchange is in the process of connecting the other branches for online real time trading, with plan for dealers to commence trading from their offices shortly.

The Security and Exchange Commission (SEC) is connected for remote surveillance of trading from its offices in Lagos and Abuja. Trading on The Exchange starts at 11.a.m. every business day and closes at about 1.30 p.m.

Pricing

Prices of new Issues are determined by Issuing Houses/Stockbrokers, while on the Secondary Market prices are determined by stockbrokers only. The market/quoted prices, along with the All-Share Index, are published daily in The Stock Exchange Daily Official List, The Nigerian Stock Exchange CAPNET (an intranet), newspapers and on the Stock Market page of the Reuters Electronic Contributor System. Our online code in the Reuters Network is NSXA-B.

Pricing and other direct controls gave way to indirect controls by the regulatory bodies (Securities and Exchange Commission and The Stock Exchange) following the deregulation of the market in 1993. Deregulation has improved the competitiveness of the market, in addition to making it more investor-friendly.

The All-Share Index

The Exchange maintains an All-Share Index formulated in January 1984 (January 3, 1984 = 100) and at present 8,930.22. Only common stocks (ordinary shares) are included in the computation of the index. The index is value-relative and is computed daily.

Clearing, Delivery and Settlement

Clearing, settlement and delivery of transactions on The Exchange are done electronically by the Central Securities Clearing System Limited (CSCS), a subsidiary of the Stock Exchange. The CSCS Limited ("the Clearing House") was incorporated in 1992 as part of the effort to make the Nigerian Stock Market more efficient and investor-friendly.

Apart from clearing, settlement, and delivery, the CSCS Limited offers custodian services.

Stock Market Legislation

Transactions in the Stock Market are guided by the following legislation, among others:

(1) Trustees Investment Act of 1990.

(2) Foreign Exchange (Miscellaneous Provisions) Act of 1995.

(3) Nigerian Investment Promotion Commission Act of 1995.

(4) Companies and Allied Matters Act of 1990

(5) Investment & Securities Act of 1999.

Regulation

Transactions on The Exchange are regulated by the Nigerian Stock Exchange, as a self-regulatory organisation (SRO), and the Securities & Exchange Commission. (SEC), which administers the Investment & Securities Act, 1999.

Foreign Investment

Following the deregulation of the capital market in 1993, the Federal Government in 1995 internationalised the capital market, with the abrogation of laws that constrained foreign participation in the Nigerian Capital Market.

Consequent upon the abrogation of the Exchange Control Act of 1962 and the Nigerian Enterprise Promotion Decree of 1989, foreigners now participate in the Nigerian Capital Market both as operators and investors. There are no limits any more to the percentage of foreign holding in any company registered in the country.

Ahead of this development, The Exchange had since June 2, 1987, linked up with the Reuters Electronic Contributor System for online global dissemination of our stock market information – trading statistics,

All-Share Index, company investment ratios, and company news (financial statements and corporate actions).

In November 1996, The Exchange launched its Intranet System (CAPNET) as one of the infrastructural support for meeting challenges of internationalisation and achieving an enhanced service delivery. CAPNET facilitates communication among local and international participants in the market.

Cable Industry in Nigeria: Opportunities, Problems and Prospects

Only 34% of the population of Nigeria has access to electricity, and its consumption per capita is barely sufficient to light a 40-watt bulb for a few hours a day. The number of telephone lines in Nigeria is only 4 per 1,000 persons as most of the lines are confined to the major urban areas. The foregoing observations point to the fact that there are enormous opportunities for cable industry expansion in Nigeria. As earlier highlighted in this chapter, the present Civilian Government in Nigeria has set a target for year 2003 to increase household access to electricity from 40% to 60% and functional telephone lines per 1,000 persons from 4 to 30.

However, cable manufacturing in Nigeria faces some basic problems which the Association of Cable Manufacturers has taken up with government in its proposal for fiscal redress in the 2001 Federal budget. The Nigerian market is awash with a large number of all types of substandard power and telephone cables imported from a number of countries, particularly from the far East. These imported substandard cables are sold at prices even lower than the raw material cost of local manufacturers.

In spite of the foregoing problems, there is good prospect for the industry in Nigeria if, and only if, the Nigerian Government is prepared to assist the industry through appropriate fiscal policies. There is now a light at the end of the tunnel to the effect that government has recently pronounced that all government departments should buy only "Made in Nigeria" goods, including cables. Efforts are being made to extend this policy to all levels of Government and indeed to the entire economy. The tariff structure in year 2001 is also in favour of cable manufacturing as import duties on raw materials for the production of all types of cables have been reduced considerably. Duties on the imported finished power and telecommunication cables which can be manufactured in Nigeria have been increased.

Nigerian Wire and Cable PLC

Nigerian Wire and Cable PLC was incorporated in 1974 to manufacture and sell electrical and telecommunication wires and cables. It was initially owned by Western State Government of Nigeria and a Japanese company, Sumitomo Electrical Industries. The company was listed in the Nigerian Stock Exchange in July 1995 and classified under Building Materials, but moved to Engineering Technology sector in 1999. The company is run by a board of thirteen Directors under the Chairmanship of Engr. (Dr) B.A. Babajide. The Managing Director and the Chief Executive Officer of the company is Engr. E.O. Adewumi, a seasoned engineer who has worked with the company for over twenty-five years. The company is presently one of the leading cable manufacturers in Nigeria, producing very high quality cable. A five-year financial summary of the company is given below:

Table 14:1
Five-Year Financial Summary

Capital Employed	1999	1998	1997	1996	1995
	'000	'000	'000	'000	'000
Turnover	409,058	351,175	217,241	190,878	122,150
Profit Before Taxation	62,311	51,034	41,170	28,515	19,150
Taxation	(17,840	(13,426	11,396	8,991	6,877
	--------	--------	--------	--------	--------
Profit After Taxation	44,471	37,658	29,774	19,524	12,616
Dividends	16,800	25,200	12,000	12,000	9,000
	--------	--------	--------	--------	--------
Retained earnings	27,553	12,457	17,774	7,524	3,618
Employment Of Funds					
Fixed Assets	69,308	63,046	51,540	39,618	43,765
Net Current Assets	201,682	180,390	179,438	68,050	56,404
	----------	----------	----------	----------	----------
Net Assets	270,682	243,436	230,978	107,668	100,172
Capital Employed					
Share Capital	84,000	84,000	60,000	30,000	30,000
Share premium account	105,336	105,336	105,336	105,336	105,336
Revaluation reserve	25,934	25,934	25,934	25,934	25,934
Reserve for Bonus Issue	–	–	24,000	12,500	7,500
Revenue reserve	55,720	28,166	15,708	9,434	6,938
	----------	----------	----------	----------	----------
Total equity (shareholders' funds)	270,990	243,436	230,978	107,668	100,172
Statistics					
Earnings per share	26.47k	22.40k	20.64k	32.54k	21.03k
Dividend per share	10k	15k	10k	20k	15k
Net worth per share	156k	145k	192	179	167k

Chapter Thirteen

The Church and Investment*

What is Investment?

Investment can be defined as an expenditure of money for income or profit. It may also mean the purchase of something of intrinsic value such as common stocks from the Capital Market, properties, painting or jewelry. Investment may also involve the commitment of funds with a view to minimising risk and safeguarding capital earning or return. This is in contrast to speculation.

When a professional investor is confronted with the expected return and risk, he or she may select assets worthy of investment using the Dominance Principle which states that among all investments with any given rate of return, the one with the least risk is the most desirable; or among all the assets in a given risk-class, the one with highest expected rate of return is the most desirable. An investor is therefore a person or institution who buys and sells financial instruments with the aim of enhancing income and/or diversifying risk. In taking a decision on what to invest upon, it must be borne in mind that the value of investments and the income derived from them can fall as well as rise.

Investment Goals

Investment goals are determined in large part by the age and socio economic status of the individual investor. For example, consider the fictitious character named Aunt Bola, a poor, little, old, frail widow,

---

A Paper presented at a seminar on "Wholeness of the Body", organised for the priests of Lagos Anglican House, at the Archbishop Vining Memorial Church, Ikeja, Lagos, on Thursday, 27th May, 1999.

who is all alone in the world and has bad nerves. Aunt Bola lives modestly on pension benefit, and the income from a small investment. She is terrified, and rightfully so, of the prospect of decrease in value of her investment. But she does not know how to manage the portfolio for herself and has no idea how many more years she will live. In order to conserve her meagre wealth, she consumes only the income from her investment and none of the principal.

In marked contrast to Aunt Bola is Tunde. Tunde is an aggressive young man who can expect a successful career (as a physician, dentist, lawyer, or scientist). Tunde's income began at a comfortable level shortly after he completed his university degree, and it can be expected to rise in years to come if he works hard. The financial future for this man is fairly secured. Tunde has different investment objectives from those of Aunt Bola. He is willing to take risks in order to gain a larger return. If his risky investments are wiped out, his family will not suffer he may merely have to work a few more years before retirement or do without some luxuries. However, Tunde is not a reckless person. He dislikes risk and is willing to assume it only because he wants the high returns, which might be attained. Thus, Aunt Bola and Tunde are both risk-averters, but Aunt Bola is the more risk-averse of the two.

Sources of Revenue for the Church

In the past, the Anglican Church used to depend on the financial resources provided by their parishioners. Such sources usually included assessment, or what is now called church maintenance dues (*owo apo Alufa*), proceeds from Sunday collections, private thanksgiving offering, Holy Communion offertory, harvest collections, proceeds from Christmas New Year and Easter thanksgiving offerings. The total income from the foregoing sources could easily sustain each church at that time because the expenditure requirements were very limited and inflation was then under control. The economic environment today has brought a greater demand on churches if they will perform all aspects of church work including evangelism and medical, as well as meet changing overheads which have become so expensive. For example, evangelism requires transportation, and other facilities to spread Christianity. The church today is expected to be involved in teaching, healing and preaching which are the three cardinal goals of Christianity. To accomplish all these require heavy financial commitments.

Realising the fact that the traditional sources of income available to the Anglican Church have become grossly inadequate to meet the expenditure needs of the Church, innovative means are employed by individual churches to meet the shortfall. I was privileged to be a member of a committee set up by the Archbishop in 1997 to examine the sources of funds for the Church. I recall that the committee submitted its report, but I wonder why it has not been adopted for use by the churches in the Diocese.

While new means of generating funds should be explored, I am of the view that the existing sources should be modified and expanded to give more revenue to the church. For example, more churches nowadays, including my own church, Bishop Adelekun Howells Memorial Church (BAHM), have developed lots of activities for the harvest season to maximise income during the season. It is observed that worshippers are more disposed to give gratitude to God during this season. Also, more churches have adopted various methods of collecting money during Sunday services either through the end of the month thanksgiving, monthly birthday and wedding anniversary thanksgiving, and various other thanksgiving activities. People are never tired to show appreciation to God at all such occasions. Tithes are now becoming very popular in Anglican Churches, but not fully tapped. There is need to create greater awareness using biblical references.

Apart from the traditional sources of revenue to the Church, the most profitable source of revenue in recent times is through the investments which individual churches can make. Investment as defined earlier can be in real estate, capital market through stocks and shares or bonds, and investment in any other form of assets which generate income for a long time. Churches in rural areas can also invest in agricultural activities, and cottage industry such as *garri* processing or rice milling.

Real Estate Development

Churches in the urban areas such as Lagos metropolis, have benefited immensely from the development of the land at their disposal. Such development may be effected through a property developer, use of a loan from a bank or any other financial institution or direct investment from savings of the Church. Churches like St. Peter's Church Faji and St. Paul's Church, Breadfruit, have taken the opportunity of their vantage locations to develop high rise office buildings which provide them with reasonable income to meet their financial obligations. Other churches with similar opportunities should explore the development of their prime land. Such move may require professional advice of estate valuers. There are certainly such experts in abundance within the Church, and they are prepared to assist. Apart from the development of office buildings, residential accommodation and shops can also be developed which can be hired out at reasonable rent.

It may also be profitable, if properly managed, for some churches to invest in economic activities such as transportation, business centres, rental services, dry cleaning and laundry services, block making, printing and bookshops. This will provide gainful employment for their members. However, such economic activities require thorough feasibility study and they should not be embarked upon until proper studies are carried out so that they do not become "a bottomless pit".

Investment in the Capital Market

Another more profitable way a church can invest its idle financial resources is to patronise the capital market also referred to as stock market in its limited definition. Investment can either be made in a new public issue of a company on the Stock Exchange usually called Initial Public Offering, (IPO), or in existing stocks through secondary market transactions. In both cases, the underlying instrument is referred to as equity securities which returns can either be in the form of dividend, capital appreciation or bonus by way of scrip. There is also long-term fixed investment that can be made in the capital market. This is called industrial loan stock for which returns are by way of fixed coupon rates which are usually more attractive than interest rates paid by banks in the money market.

Why Invest in the Stock-Market?

You may already be a share owner without realising it; most life assurance companies and pension fund managers invest their customers' money in the stock market.

Investing or dealing in shares can be risky, particularly in the short term. If the company you buy its shares does badly, you could lose most or all of your money. However, the potential gains are higher than with other forms of investment, provided you hold for a reasonable length of time. In many developed countries, since the Second World War, two forms of long-term investment have done better than all others: property investment and share ownership (although the recent recession has, of course, taken its toll on property values).

What Exactly is a Share?

A share confers part ownership of a company offered for sale to the public. The company is able to raise cash for expansion and new ventures by selling its shares to investors. Some companies – family business, for example – do not trade their shares. Firms that do are known as Public Limited Companies (plc), and seek a listing on the Stock Exchange, which at present is the market for the shares of more than 300 firms. The first time it 'goes public' (also known as a flotation), a company will often announce its intentions with advertisements in the press. This is called an 'Offer for Sale' or Public Subscription.

What Do You Get as a Shareholder?

As a shareholder, you are a part owner of the company, entitled to take part in its decisions. You are sent an annual company report; you can vote on company issues; and you have the right to attend shareholders' meetings, like the **Annual General Meeting** (AGM). If the company is doing well and profits rise, you benefit. Your shares should be worth more than when you bought them; and you may receive an income called dividend, as well as participate in the rights issued by the company.

How Shares Can Make Money for You

A share's value is not fixed. Its price is determined by many factors: the company's recent performance; the state of the economy the company trades in; national and international economic and political changes; the level of consumer demand; and the peculiarly unpredictable human factors of confidence and pessimism.

If you buy a share at one price and sell it at a higher price, you make a profit; if you sell it at a lower price, you incur a loss. Shares can provide an income (though not necessarily a regular one) through the payment of dividends. However, a company can choose not to pay dividend at all, by investing any profits back into the company. Dividends are usually paid once a year, but few companies in Nigeria pay twice, the **Interim Dividend** and the **Final Dividend**. The company deducts withholding tax at the rate specified by the government, currently ten per cent, before paying shareholders.

A company's shares will sometimes show a rise in value just before the dividend dates, since the imminent income is attractive to buyers. The price is usually brought back into line just after the dividend has been paid. There is an easy way of telling whether a share is available with or without a dividend payment; **cumdiv** means that the buyer will get the dividend, **exdiv** means that the seller will be taking it.

What is a Stock

Strictly speaking, the term stock is used for Stock Market holdings, which pay a fixed rate of interest (like gilts). However, in day-to-day parlance, the words stocks, shares, equities and securities mean pretty much the same thing.

Ordinary Shares

As a private investor in the Stock Market, what you will almost always be dealing with are known as Ordinary Shares. You may come across some other types of shares. These include preference shares.

Preference Shares

These shares earn a fixed dividend income. The owners are entitled to receive dividends before the holders of ordinary shares. If a company is wound up, preference shareholders are paid first, once all the creditors have been paid in full.

Unlisted Securities

Companies which are not big enough for a Stock Exchange listing, or which do not wish to pay for listing, can be traded on the Secondary Market, the Unlisted Securities Market (USM). The USM shares are highly volatile, but this type of market is not yet available in Nigeria. However, the Nigeria Stock Exchange (NSE), has what is called Second-Tier Market for small companies with less stringent listing requirement.

Buying Shares

Finding a Stockbroker

To buy shares, you need to contact a stockbroker. Some stockbrokers will simply buy and sell shares at your request. This is called Dealing Only or Execution Only. Stockbrokers are allowed to charge up to 2.75% brokerage commission. You can ask a stockbroker for advice on what to buy and sell. This is an Advisory Service for which a fee can be charged. Or, if you prefer to let your stockbroker buy and sell your shares "**portfolio management**" without having to discuss every deal, you may choose a **discretionary service**, where your stockbroker simply sends you a regular statement, showing what has been bought and sold.

Choosing Your Shares

When you give a stockbroker an order to buy or sell shares, that order is binding; so if you use a Dealing Only service, you must be absolutely sure of what you want. For steady, long-term investment, you should consider 'blue chip' shares. These are the shares of secure and respected companies, many of which are household names: for example, LBN, PZ, Cadbury, Mobil, Nestle, FBN and AIICO. The term 'blue chip' derives from the highest-value chip in a game of poker. You are unlikely to see spectacularly fast rises in their share prices, but it is likely that over a number of years, they will earn steady profits for their shareholders. Apart from 'blue chip' companies, other stock classifications are:

(i)   Income stocks – stocks that pay dividends higher than the average dividend payment in the market.

(ii)   Growth stocks – stocks with an above-average growth rate in earnings and

(iii) Cyclical stocks – whose prices go up and down with the business cycles.

Whatever type of shares you are looking for, you should start to read the financial pages of daily newspaper. It can also be helpful to talk to friends or colleagues about how they chose any shares that they own. Remember, though, that the past records of a company cannot be taken as a guarantee for its future success.

Summary of Discussion

As earlier defined, investment is the act of committing funds to a project with a view to minimising risk and maximising return. The ability to identify optimum investment vehicle lies at the heart of investment decision. Financial security, wealth and success are the products of diligence and thoughtfulness. The combination of hard work and wise decision making, if applied to opportunity, results in prosperity. Our churches need to be more business-like in resource mobilisation, realising the fact that it is becoming more and more difficult to raise revenue from what used to be the traditional revenue sources. As we move towards the new millennium, boundless opportunities exist within the economy and these should be exploited to meet the challenges ahead of the church to foster evangelism and meet the demands of the 21st Century church.

In assigning priority to various types of investment vehicles, the effect of inflation must be put into consideration. Interest rates have fallen to very low levels except recently when the Central Bank of Nigeria (CBN) significantly increased the rate payable on Government Treasury Bills, which is now about 19%. Whether this will be a permanent feature is another thing to consider. Returns from properties and land have been relatively poor in recent times. Equities, however, have performed relatively well and over the long term beaten inflation, bank and mortgage deposits. To maximise returns from the various types of investment, each church should have investment committee made up of parishioners with good financial and business background who will provide regular advice and manage the portfolio for the church. An investment policy should be formulated which takes cognisance of the return requirements and risk tolerance of the church. It must also reflect the liquidity requirements, the investment horizon and other unique needs of the church.

Index

193